SpringerBriefs in Finance

More information about this series at http://www.springer.com/series/10282

Linda Peters

Real Options Illustrated

Springer

Linda Peters
Applied Economics
University of Antwerp
Antwerp, Belgium

ISSN 2193-1720 ISSN 2193-1739 (electronic)
SpringerBriefs in Finance
ISBN 978-3-319-28309-8 ISBN 978-3-319-28310-4 (eBook)
DOI 10.1007/978-3-319-28310-4

Library of Congress Control Number: 2016931340

Printed on acid-free paper

This Springer imprint is published by Springer Nature
The registered company is Springer International Publishing AG Switzerland

Contents

About the Author

Linda Peters is PhD Candidate in the field of Applied Economics at the University of Antwerp. As a PhD candidate, she is involved in the application of Real Options theory to Global Public Policy and her research contributes to bridge the gap between theory and practice. Her research interests include Real Options, Global Public Policy, Social Protection, Models of Decision-Making, and Probability Distributions.

Introduction

Large investment projects with a long time horizon are subject to many internal (i.e., technical) and external (i.e., market) uncertainties. In a process of project evaluation, practitioners traditionally use capital budgeting techniques, such as net present value, decision tree-, scenario- and sensitivity analysis. Unfortunately, these methods cannot fully quantify these uncertainties. Real options analysis (ROA) does provide the necessary tools and techniques to deal with uncertainty and is much appreciated as a complement to traditional valuation methods.

ROA literature is usually filled to the brim with partial differential equations, probability density functions and simulation techniques, which is supposed to convince us of the added value of ROA. Unfortunately, practitioners are not convinced about the applicability of ROA. They experience difficulties regarding the implementation of the method and perceive ROA as a black box. This has not been much of a surprise since ROA is complex and incorporates many restrictive assumptions. So, how can we prevent ROA to be just another forgotten paradigm in the world of finance?

Standard ROA literature usually incorporates the headlines of the methodology, whereas practitioners seek for an in-depth explanation in order to reproduce and apply it to their own field. We believe this is the key to improve the accessibility of ROA for practitioners. Therefore, this book explains the standard ROA literature step by step, without the use of complex math. Practitioners are provided with a real options framework and are encouraged to study the methodology in-depth instead of giving up after reading the introduction. The reader will have a better grasp about how ROA works and will be able to provide his or her judgment about ROA, since all the basics of ROA and its pros and cons are discussed in this book.

Don't expect to be an expert of ROA or to develop new and complex ROA methodologies after reading this book. However, you are sufficiently equipped with the ROA basics and its framework, which enables you to perform independent future research. From this, you can judge whether or not ROA is of any value to your field. We wish you good luck and have fun while reading this introductory book about Real Options Analysis.

This book is structured as follows. Chapter 1 discusses the basic concepts of real options analysis. Chapter 2 provides a comparative study between real options and other traditional capital budgeting techniques and from this it is shown that traditional valuation models cannot capture the flexibility to adapt an investment decision in response to the uncertainty. Chapter 3 discusses the most widely used real option models in an accessible way and also highlights the important strengths and weaknesses of these models. Chapter 4 explains and addresses the importance to study the impact of probability distributions on real options valuation. Chapter 5, the final chapter, provides a glossary of terms that are commonly used on the field of real options.

Chapter 1
Introduction to Real Options Analysis

This chapter provides an introduction to the real options way of thinking. The valuation methods of real options are based on the option pricing theory for financial securities. Therefore in the first part of this chapter the basic concepts of financial options will be discussed. Real Options Analysis apply these basic concepts to real or physical assets. The second part of this chapter commences with the translation of financial to real option theory. Thereafter, a simple example is presented to illustrate the use of option pricing to value a deferral option and to describe the strengths and weaknesses of real options. In the concluding part, different option valuation methods such as dynamic programming, contingent claims and Monte Carlo simulation, are discussed.

1.1 Options

Real options provide decision makers the opportunity to make and capitalize on emerging opportunities during the lifetime of the project. Decision makers have the choice to defer, expand or cease an investment project. These opportunities suddenly can become available, cease to exist or be enforced. Decision makers are responsible for making the right decision, i.e. the decision that maximizes the potential value of the project and reduces the downside risk. The value of the project is defined in terms of cash. In order to select the best project, decision makers will estimate the value of the embedded options in the project and select the one with the highest option value. Crucial to the valuation of options is uncertainty or volatility. This fundamental parameter complicates the valuation of real options, but at the same it adds significant value to projects. Real options acknowledges the value of uncertainty in investment decisions and provides solutions for handling these uncertainties. Unfortunately, decision makers who only use traditional capital budgeting techniques often underestimate or ignore the extent of uncertainty and its implications.

L. Peters, *Real Options Illustrated*, SpringerBriefs in Finance,
DOI 10.1007/978-3-319-28310-4_1

Real option reasoning is a heuristic based on the logic of financial options. Therefore, this section starts with the basics of financial option valuation and thereafter translates it to the principles of real option valuation.

1.1.1 Basics of Option Theory

In finance, an option is a contract which gives the owner the right, but not the obligation, to buy or sell an underlying asset at a specified price on or before a specified date. Options can be created on almost any asset, such as stocks, bonds or currencies. The price at which the underlying asset can be purchased or sold is called the exercise price or strike price and is determined at the time the option contract is formed. The owner has the right to determine whether or not to exercise the option. The option will only be exercised whenever it's profitable to do so. The payoff of the option when it's not exercised equals zero. In other words, the payoff of the option cannot be negative, apart from the option premium.

1.1.1.1 Call Option and Put Option

There are two types of options: calls and puts. A call option on a stock gives the buyer or holder the right (but not the obligation) to buy the stock at a particular price within a specified period of time. For example, if you buy a 1-week European call option (exercised at expiration) on a stock with an exercise price of $30, you will have the right to buy from the option's seller one stock for the exercise price of $30 at expiration (after 1 week), irrespective of the stock's price at that time. Suppose the stock goes up to $50 at the time the call expires, then you will be able to exercise the call to buy the stock for $30 and immediately sell it in the market for $50. The stock price rise to $50 represents a profit of $50 − $30 = $20, in other words the call's payoff equals $20: the option has intrinsic value. In this case a call option is said to be in-the-money, i.e. when the exercise price is lower than the stock price. If the stock price decreases to $15, you will not exercise the option, since this will result in a loss. The option has no intrinsic value, the minimum payoff is zero, and therefore the option is said to be out-of-the-money.

Determining the value of the option is crucial for the buyer to decide whether or not to buy the call. One of the primary determinants of option value is the volatility. These issues play a key role in Real Options Analysis.

The second type of option is a put option. A put option gives the holder the right to sell the stock at a particular price within a specified period of time. A put option can be viewed as the opposite of a call option.

1.1.1.2 Long Position and Short Position

In the previous example we have introduced the buyer of the call option. This is also referred to as the investor who has taken the long position (i.e. has bought the option). The seller or writer of the option takes a short position. This means that the investor has sold or written the option. The seller of an option receives cash up front, but has potential liabilities later. The seller's profit or loss is the reverse of that for the buyer of the option. It's a so-called zero-sum game.

1.1.1.3 American Option and European Option

Another important distinction in options terminology is between an American and a European option. With an American option you have the right to exercise the option at any time during its life. European options give you the right to exercise an option only at the end of its life. Options traded on option markets are usually American options, whereas non-traded options are usually European.

1.1.1.4 The Basic Idea of Valuation

Option value plays a key role when an investor has to decide whether or not to buy or sell an option. Even though several methods have been developed to value an option, the underlying concept is the same for each method and is as follows. A company creates value by investing only in projects where the (discounted) project inflows outweigh the (discounted) project outflows. Market (present) value is defined as the future sum of cash flows given a specified rate of return, where future cash flows are discounted at the discount rate. This basic concept is essential in Real Option Valuation and the challenge is to determine the market (present) value of the expected cash inflows.

1.1.1.5 Hedging

Another key concept in financial theory and often applied to the valuation of options is hedging. Hedging is a way of reducing risk, such as the risk in a project, by one or more transactions in the financial markets. A hedge can be constructed from many types of financial instruments such as futures and options. A future is a bilateral contract (as is the case with options) that allows one party, the seller, to sell a particular reference asset at a forward price for settlement at a future date, and the second party, the buyer, to purchase the reference asset at the forward price on a named date. The difference between futures and options is that a future contract is a legal obligation to both counterparties, one to deliver and the other to accept the delivery. In real options analysis a hedge is constructed from an option. Therefore, only this type of hedging is discussed and illustrated with an example of Hull (2009).

Let's suppose we own 1,000 Microsoft shares at the current price of $28 per share. We expect that the price of the Microsoft share will drop dramatically and therefore we need to hedge against such a price decrease. Our hedge involves the purchase of 10 put options for the month July at the strike price of $27.50 in order to have the right to sell 1,000 shares at a price of $27.50 per share. If the price of the put option is $100, the cost of the hedging strategy will be 10 × $100 = $1,000. This means a guarantee of at least $27.50 per Microsoft share. If the stock price exceeds the $27.50, the option will not be exercised since it has no value. By doing this, we have taken a hedging position for a price guarantee of $1,000 against a maximum potential exposure of 1,000 × ($28 – $27.50) = $500.

1.1.2 From Financial Options to Real Options

In the previous section we've introduced the fundamental essence of financial options. The basic characteristics of these financial options could be recognized in real-life investment projects. For example the opportunity to sell an investment project is equivalent to a put option. The equivalent of a financial option with regard to real-life investment projects are real options. 'Real' refers to real-life investment projects or physical assets in comparison to the 'intangible' financial options. Real options are generally distinguished from financial options in that they are not typically traded as securities. However, real options are modelled in such a way as if they are traded.

A real option gives the right, but not the obligation, to take different courses of action (for example to defer, abandon or expand) with respect to real assets at a predetermined price at a certain time in the future. Real Options Analysis supports managers to formulate and obtain their strategic objectives and maximize the value of the shareholders or investors.

Copeland and Antikarov (2001) lists five essential key levers of real options and add an important sixth lever:

1. The value of the underlying asset or stock price. The underlying asset of a real option is a project, investment or an acquisition. If the value of the underlying asset increases, the real option value, when it's equivalent to a call option, increases as well. Conversely, if the value of the underlying asset increases, the value of a put option decreases. Real options are generally distinguished from financial options in that the owner of the real option has the ability to influence the value of the underlying asset, whereas this is not possible with regard to financial options.
2. Exercise price or investment cost. The exercise price is the premium paid for acquiring the asset (with a call option) and in case of a put option it is the premium received for selling the asset. As the exercise price of an option

increases, the value of the call option decreases and the value of the put increases.
3. Time to expiration of the option. As the time to expiration increases, so does the option value.
4. The standard deviation of the value of the underlying risky asset or volatility. The higher the volatility or riskiness of the underlying risky asset, the greater the value of the real option. This is true for both calls and puts, because the payoffs of an option depend on the difference between the value of the underlying and the exercise price and the likelihood of this increases with the volatility of the underlying.
5. The risk-free rate of interest over de life time of an option. Increases in the interest rate will increase the value of calls and reduce the value of puts.
6. Dividends paid of the underlying asset. Dividends on the underlying stock have the effect of reducing the price of a call option and increase the price of a put option.

1.1.3 Common Real Options

The previous section has introduced a theoretical framework of real options. The main question is: how to deal with these theoretical concepts in practice? What are the common types of real options? (Brach 2003). In this section we'll discuss the most common types of real options and the overview of Smit and Trigeorgis (2004) will serve as a basis for this discussion. The common types of real options are:

- Option to defer
- Option to expand or contract
- Option to abandon or switch

These options are called simple options. More advanced type of options, such as compound or growth options, are variations on simple options. For these type of options, the option value depends on the value of other options: option on an option. Compound options are similar to growth options, but while growth options concentrate on phase-expansions of the already developed project, compound options apply to projects that have multiple investment phases. Other advanced options are barrier and rainbow options. This section will focus on the simple options.

1.1.3.1 Option to Defer

A firm has the option to defer or to postpone an investment until it has more information about the project in the future, such as information about market developments. This option has much value in situations with the simultaneous existence of uncertainty and irreversibility of the project. The option to defer is analogous to an American call option on the gross present value of the completed project's operating cash flows, with the exercise price being equal to investment costs of the project.

Deferral options are suitable for proprietary investments in markets with high-entry barriers such as patents or requirements of specific or unique knowledge. Deferral options are especially valuable in resource extraction industries, farming, paper products and real estate development because of the high uncertainty, long-term investment horizon and limited competition.

1.1.3.2 Option to Expand or Contract

Once a firm has invested in a project, it could adjust the decision regarding this project. For example the, firm could expand its current business activities by acquiring its competitor. This is equivalent to an American call option on the value of the additional capacity and the exercise price on this call is equivalent to the cost of creating the additional business activities discounted to the time of option exercise. In Chap. 3 a practical example of an expansion option will be discussed by using the Portes Case developed by Copeland and Antikarov (2001). Portes Inc. uses the expansion option to make further investments and increase the internet sales.

A firm could also decide to reduce the scale of a project's operation, when a project does not meet the output expectations. It's an American put option on the value of the lost capacity. The exercise price is the present value of the future expenditures saved as seen at the time of exercise the option.

Expansion and contraction options are popular options with the introduction of new products in uncertain markets. These options provide opportunities for firms to adapt to the changing markets.

1.1.3.3 Option to Abandon or Switch

Firms also have the option to abandon existing projects, when the project circumstances become unfavourable. This is called an abandonment option. It often saves firms a great deal of money. In Chap. 3 this option will be discussed in the Portes Case by Copeland and Antikarov (2001). Portes Inc. uses the abandonment option to sell an entire internet platform.

A firm could also have the option to switch the resources from one project to another project. Usually, the firm abandons the original project and at the same time starts a new project. The option to switch is a complex option, because a decision has to be taken between two interdependent projects that are both facing lots of uncertainty.

The option to abandon and option to switch are American put options on the project's value. The underlying value of these options is the expected value of the cash inflows of the project. The exercise price of these options is the liquidation (or resale) value of the project less any closing-down costs. In case of a switching option the exercise price is equal to the costs of switching from moving one resource to another.

Abandonment options mitigate the impact of very poor investment outcomes and increase the initial valuation of a project. Abandonment and switching options are particularly important for large capital intense projects. They are especially valuable with the introduction of new products in uncertain markets, projects where it's easy to switch from one to the other resource or products that serve multiple markets.

1.2 A Simple Real Options Analysis Example

After reading the previous section, we are now familiar with the basic concepts of real options. This section illustrates the application of real options principles based on the example of the book *Investment under Uncertainty* (1994) written by Avinash Dixit and Robert Pindyck.

Suppose we consider to invest in a widget factory. This investment is completely irreversible, in other words the widget factory can only produce widgets and cannot be used for other purposes. The investment for the factory is $1, 600 and the factory is able to produce one widget per year without operating costs. At the moment the price of a widget is $200, but this could change next year. There is a probability of 50 % that after 1 year the widget's price will rise to $300 and a probability of 50 % that the widget's price will fall to $100. After 2 years the widget's price will remain constant. In case of a last years' price increase, the widget's price after 2 years will remain $300, and in case of a price decrease, the widget's price will remain $100. We assume a 10 % discount rate to calculate the present value of the expected cash flows. The main question is whether or not to invest in the widget factory and if so, whether to invest in the factory right now or to wait for example 1 year until more information becomes available about the price fluctuations of the widget.

Suppose we decide to invest today, the Net Present Value (NPV), which is the difference between the expected present value of the cash inflows minus the expected present value of the cash outflows, could be calculated. This will result in a NPV of $600, given that the initial investment is $1,600 and the expected future price for each year equals $ 200. The NPV is calculated as follows:

$$
\begin{aligned}
NPV_{invest\ now} &= present\ value \ - \ initial\ costs \\
&= \sum_{t=0}^{\infty} \frac{200}{(1+10\%)^t} - 1{,}600 \\
&= 2{,}200 - 1{,}600 = \$600
\end{aligned}
$$

In the previous example, the sum formula for geometric series has been used to calculate $\sum_{t=0}^{\infty} \frac{200}{(1+10\%)^t}$. A geometric series is an infinite series and uses the following standard notation: $a \times \sum_{t=0}^{\infty} r^t$. If $-1 < r < 1$, the result of the geometric series is $a \times \frac{1}{1-r}$. The geometric series is $\sum_{t=0}^{\infty} \frac{200}{(1+10\%)^t}$ and can be written as $200 \times \sum_{t=0}^{\infty} \frac{1}{(1+10\%)^t}$ and will result in a geometric series with a = 200, $r = \frac{1}{1.10}$. Given that $-1 < r < 1$, we apply the sum rule and from this it follows that the sum equals $200 \times \left[\frac{1}{1 - {}^{1}\!/_{1.10}}\right]$.

$$
\begin{aligned}
\sum_{t=0}^{\infty} \frac{200}{(1+10\%)^t} &= 200 \times \sum_{t=0}^{\infty} \frac{1}{(1+10\%)^t} \\
&= 200 \times \left[\frac{1}{1 - {}^{1}\!/_{1.10}}\right] \\
&= 200 \times \left[\frac{1}{1 - {}^{10}\!/_{11}}\right] \\
&= 200 \times \left[\frac{1}{{}^{1}\!/_{11}}\right] \\
&= 200 \times 11 \\
&= \$2{,}200
\end{aligned}
$$

What will be the NPV if the investment is deferred until the end of a year? We decide not to invest if the price decreases and only exercise the deferral option if the price increases to \$ 300. The NPV of the project including the deferral option is calculated in a similar way as the NPV without deferral option. However in case of the deferral option the geometric series starts at $t = 1$ and not $t = 0$, since the investment is deferred until the end of year 1. We'll have to determine $\sum_{t=1}^{\infty} \frac{300}{(1+10\%)^t}$, but we cannot simply use the sum formula for the geometric series, since the sum formula only applies when the geometric series starts at $t = 0$. However, this can be solved as follows:

$$
\sum_{t=0}^{\infty} \frac{300}{(1+10\%)^t} = \frac{300}{(1+10\%)^0} + \sum_{t=1}^{\infty} \frac{300}{(1+10\%)^t}
$$

It follows that

$$\sum_{t=1}^{\infty}\frac{300}{(1+10\%)^t} = \sum_{t=0}^{\infty}\frac{300}{(1+10\%)^t} - \frac{300}{(1+10\%)^0}$$
$$= \sum_{t=0}^{\infty}\frac{300}{(1+10\%)^t} - 300$$

Using this equation, we can use the sum formula of the geometric series in order to determine

$$\sum\nolimits_{t=0}^{\infty}\frac{300}{(1+10\%)^t}.$$

Since we have figured out how to determine $\sum\nolimits_{t=1}^{\infty}\frac{300}{(1+10\%)^t}$, the NPV for the deferral option can be calculated when the geometric series starts at $t = 1$. This results in a NPV of \$773:

$$\begin{aligned}
NPV_{\textit{invest next year}} &= 0.5 \times \left(\sum_{t=1}^{\infty}\frac{300}{(1+10\%)^t} - \frac{1{,}600}{1.10}\right)\\
&= 0.5 \times \left(\sum_{t=0}^{\infty}\frac{300}{(1+10\%)^t} - 300 - \frac{1{,}600}{1.10}\right)\\
&= 0.5 \times \left(300 \times 11 - 300 - \frac{1{,}600}{1.10}\right)\\
&= 0.5 \times \left(3000 - \frac{1{,}600}{1.10}\right)\\
&= 850/1.1\\
&= \$773
\end{aligned}$$

We are better off by deciding today to defer, rather than to invest. The value of waiting to decide results in a NPV of \$773, whereas investing results in a NPV of \$600. Therefore the value of the deferral option equals \$773 − \$600 = \$173. This additional flexibility enables us to wait and see the result of the change in price and respond to these uncertainties accordingly. In other words, to invest when the price increases and do nothing in case the price decreases.

1.3 Key Strengths of Real Options Analysis

Real Options Analysis acknowledges the fact that many projects contain embedded options and provides adequate tooling to incorporate and correctly value these options. This is a problem with the traditional NPV approach. NPV does not consider these options in the decision-making process, and therefore underestimates flexibility of projects and assumes that the results of these projects are static and that decisions of these projects are irreversible. Real options analysis does capture the value of managerial flexibility to adapt and revise decisions in response to unexpected market decisions. And therefore real options analysis maximizes potential gains and minimizes downside losses. Incorporating options and managerial flexibility to deal with these options into the valuation process results in a higher project value than with traditional capital valuation techniques. Projects that are rejected with these traditional approaches are accepted and are considered as valuable with the use of real options because of the acknowledgement of flexibility. This is illustrated in the examples of this book.

1.4 Weaknesses of Real Options Analysis

This section addresses the general criticisms on Real Options Analysis and provides the underlying thoughts of these criticisms in Chap. 3 Real option methods illustrated.

The first criticism on real option analysis comes from practitioners who often find real options difficult to understand and to implement due to the complex mathematics involved (He 2007). The simple example presented in Sect. 1.1 already involves some complex math. These practitioners prefer to stick to the traditional valuation methods because of its simplicity. Managers simply feel confused by implementing a method they perceive as a black box, and why should they use tools they do not fully understand?

Real Options Analysis is a heuristic based on the logic of financial options. However, the assumptions that are applicable to financial option valuation do not necessarily apply to real options. A consequence of this is that these models tend to reflect perfection rather than economic reality (Triantis 2005, Collan 2011), which creates a gap between theory and practice. An example of such an unrealistic assumption is the choice of a stochastic process for the underlying asset price when using the Black-Scholes model. Black-Scholes is a mathematical model based on the notion that the stock price follows a random walk. The question however remains whether it is justifiable to use such an assumption for real-life situations. These types of disputable assumptions could question the credibility of such a method.

Another criticism also concerns the gap between theory and practice. Sanders et al. (2013) argues that even though a deferral option is a preferred solution in theory, in practice this is not always the case, taking into account projects where investors need to compete in order to obtain a project, such as a tender. The wait-and-see approach might not be the most optimal solution, since timing is crucial in these kind of situations. In these situations there is not always time to wait, because a competitor might act faster and in that case the opportunity of obtaining a profitable project might be lost. Furthermore, gathering information could require such a huge investment that doesn't add any value to gather more information again.

1.5 Three Approaches

There are several approaches to real options pricing and each approach contains several methods that addresses real options problems in a different way. These approaches are categorized as follows, and are applied to a broader scope than only Real Options Analysis:

- Dynamic programming
- Contingent claims
- Monte Carlo simulation

Each approach will be discussed in the following sections, but prior to this, an important distinction between methods in general is discussed: the difference between analytical and numerical methods.

1.5.1 Analytical Versus Numerical

Models are used to simulate real-life situations. The essence of modeling is to replace the situation or project under study by a simple object that describes the real system and/or its behavior. These real life problems are solved by using mathematical techniques, where the essence of the real-life problem is expressed in mathematical notations such as a set of mathematical equations. There are two ways to solve these kind of mathematical problems: analytically and numerically. If the solution for the set of equations is found through the use of mathematical methods such as calculus, trigonometry, and other techniques, it is called an analytical solution. This is also referred to as a *closed-form solution.*

However, real-life situations are often too complex and therefore the math simply becomes too complicated to solve analytically. In that case we turn to numerical methods, which are used when no formula is available. Numerical methods provide approximate solutions, for instance by repeated simulations and draw conclusions from these simulations. Other numerical methods reduce analytical equations in such a way that they could be solved. A number of analytical methods, such as Black-Scholes, have been developed for financial options. Unfortunately, Black-Scholes is limited in its use and therefore numerical methods have become more popular.

1.5.2 Dynamic Programming

Dynamic programming is a method for solving complex problems by breaking them down into simpler sub-problems. A capital budget decision consists of a sequence of decisions, called stages (instead of one comprehensive decision), where each stage produces an optimal solution. Because of the interdependency between the different stages, the decision at one stage has a direct consequence on the decision made at the next stage. The entire process of consecutive decisions is divided into two parts at each point of time: the immediate decision, and the remaining decisions, all of whose results are consolidated in the continuation value. To determine the profit-maximizing decision we work backwards from the terminal nodes to the initial node. At these terminal nodes, there is no continuation value and therefore it's easy to determine the optimal choice. Moving from the terminal nodes to the previous (intermediate) nodes, we compare the expected continuation value with the current value and choose the best option for the previous (intermediate) nodes. This is also referred to as backward-induction technique.

If this stage procedure is modeled with time as a continuous variable, the equation will result in a partial differential equation, the Bellman equation, also called the fundamental equation of optimality. In case of an infinite time horizon, there is no value for the last decision point to work backwards from. This shouldn't be a problem, since the Bellman-equation transforms into a recursive equation. A special property of this recursive Bellman-equation is that it returns a better guess than the initial guess we provide as input for the Bellman-equation. By repeating this procedure several times, the equation will converge to the solution. Dynamic programming is therefore also applicable to situations in case of infinite time horizons.

Dynamic programming problems are often solved by partial differential equations, which can become very complex and their analytical solutions are even more complex. A way to avoid these complex procedures is to model time as a discrete variable instead of a continuous variable and to solve the dynamic programming problem numerically. A simple example of this was illustrated in Sect. 1.1 of this book. The scope of this book is limited to numerical dynamic programming and therefore complex partial differential equations will not be further discussed. An example of such a numerical method is the method of Cox et al. (1979), which will be discussed in this book.

1.5.3 Contingent Claims

In financial theory a contingent claim is a claim of which the value depends on, i.e. is contingent upon, the value of an asset, the underlying asset Buckley et al. (1998). If the payoffs of a new asset can be replicated through a portfolio of existing traded assets, the value of this new asset can be determined. In this case both the value of the new asset and the value of the portfolio are the same, because of similar risk and return characteristics. When a discrepancy arises between the two values, arbitrageurs will take advantage of this opportunity by purchasing the cheaper one of the assets or portfolios, repackaging it, and immediately selling it on a different market at a higher price. Because of these arbitrage opportunities, the mispricing of the new asset compared to the portfolio will be resolved over a certain period of time, i.e. the no-arbitrage situation. There are two ways to create a replicating portfolio of the new asset, through the risk-neutral and replicating portfolio approaches. Both methods of the contingent claims approach will be discussed in this book.

The contingent claims is a frequently used approach, such as with the method of Copeland and Antikarov (2001), and has been applied for the first time by Black and Scholes (1973).

1.5.4 Comparing Dynamic Programming and Contingent Claims

Under restrictive assumptions, dynamic programming and contingent claims result in a similar solution for investment value through the use of another differential equation. However, the basic assumptions of both approaches differ. One of the important differences is the treatment of the discount factor for the valuation of cash flows by decision makers. Dynamic programming involves the adoption of an exogenous discount rate that reflects the opportunity cost of capital for investment projects of similar risk. Contingent claims only considers the risk free rate to be exogenous. In practice of dynamic programming this discount rate is assumed to be constant for simplicity, whereas in reality this will not be constant. Therefore, a constant discount rate is somewhat arbitrary and hard to verify. Accordingly, contingent claims provides a better treatment of the discount rate.

However, contingent claims require the existence of a sufficiently set of rich markets in risky assets. This enables a perfect replication of the stochastic component of the risky asset and is very demanding. This is not a requirement under the dynamic programming approach. If the risk cannot be derived from assets in the market, an arbitrary discount rate can be used instead.

According to Insley and Wirjanto (2008) the contingent claim approach is preferred to the dynamic programming approach for the application of real options in practice. This is to avoid unnecessary complex calculations for the correct stochastic discount rate.

1.5.5 Monte Carlo Simulation

A crucial variable in Real Options Analysis is volatility. We will demonstrate that in Real Options Analysis, the higher the volatility, the higher the real option value. However, the volatility also increases the complexity of the real options model. Therefore, in most cases it is impossible to solve a real options problem with closed form solutions. This is especially the case when a model incorporates different types of uncertainties. In these types of situations we will not look for a closed form solution, but will simulate the volatility. For example, the impact of price changes on the turnover is performed through simulations. The simulation results from a wide range of different scenarios provide us an indication about all the possible solutions of a given situation.

Calculations for a given scenario in the context of real options include the fluctuation of the price of the underlying value of the option over time. The value of the option depends on its underlying value, which is based on several market variables. There are several approaches to determine the option value. One of them is to relate the option value to both the current underlying value and to the time path of the price fluctuation until that current underlying value. This is a problem for the dynamic programming approach, since this approach uses backward-induction, i.e. process of reasoning backwards in time. On the contrary this won't be a problem with the Monte Carlo simulation approach, because the calculations are performed from the beginning of a problem or situation. Another method to determine the option value is to take the average underlying value for the entire period of time. Again, this won't be a problem for Monte Carlo, because the calculations for a complete scenario are performed first and therefore the average underlying value is determined per scenario before the calculation of the option value. The major advantage of Monte Carlo is its wide applicability, because Monte Carlo is applicable to situations where the value of the option is path-dependent or dependent on the end values of the underlying value. Another important advantage of Monte Carlo simulation is that any stochastic process for the underlying asset can be constructed with this approach and is not restricted to the well-known random walk.

A disadvantage of the Monte Carlo method is its difficulties with the early exercise of options, because the Monte Carlo approach performs the calculations of the scenario before calculating the option value. Therefore evaluating the option value of early exercise creates problems.

Another important drawback of the Monte Carlo approach is its computational expense. Nowadays, with the high-end technology, i.e. computers and tooling such as Crystal Ball © or @Risk ©, the Monte Carlo method is a very promising method for the analysis of real options. Copeland and Antikarov (2001) and Datar and Mathews (2007) use the Monte Carlo method to model volatility, both in a different way. Also, de Neufville et al. (2006) incorporates simulation techniques to determine the stochastic component of demand.

References

Black F, Scholes M (1973) The pricing of options and corporate liabilities. J Polit Econ 81 (3) (May–Jun):637–654

Brach MA (2003) Real options in practice. Wiley, Hoboken, New Jersey

Buckley A, Ross SA, Westerfield RW, Jaffe JF (1998) Corporate finance Europe. McGraw-Hill, Maidenhead

Collan M (2011) Thoughts about selected models for the valuation of real options. Mathematica 50 (2):5–12

Copeland T, Antikarov V (2001) Real options a practitioners guide. TEXERE, New York/London

Cox JC, Ross SA, Rubinstein M (1979) Option pricing: a simplified approach. J Financ Econ 7:229–263

Datar VT, Mathews SH (2007) A practical method for valuing real options: the Boeing approach. J Appl Corp Finance 19(2):95–104, Spring 2007

He Y (2007) Real options in the energy markets. http://doc.utwente.nl/58482/1/thesis_He.pdf. Accessed 12 Jan 2014

Hull JC (2009) Options, futures and other derivatives, 7th edn. Pearson Prentice Hall, New Jersey

Insley M, Wirjanto T (2008) Contrasting two approaches in real options valuation contingent claims versus dynamic programming. J Forest Econ 16(2):157–176

de Neufville R, Scholtes S, Wang T (2006) Real options by spreadsheet: parking garage case example. ASCE J Infrastruct Syst 12(2):107–111

Pindyck R, Dixit A (1994) Investing under uncertainty. Princeton University Press, Princeton

Sanders M, Fuss S, Engelen PJ (2013) Mobilizing private funds for carbon capture and storage: an exploratory field study in the Netherlands. Int J Greenh Gas Con 19:595–605

Smit HTJ, Trigeorgis L (2004) Strategic investment. Real options and games. Princeton University Press, Princeton/Oxford

Triantis A (2005) Realizing the potential of real options does theory meet practice. J Appl Cor Finance 17(2):8–16, Spring 2005

Chapter 2
Comparison of Real Options Analysis and Other Methods

This chapter offers a comparison of the real options valuation approach, using the contingent claims approach, to two traditional valuation methods. The first traditional valuation approach discussed in this chapter is the NPV analysis, which also includes the contingent claims approach and the second is the decision tree analysis. Through this comparative study, it is shown when real options provide better results than traditional approaches. This will be illustrated on the basis of Copeland and Antikarov (2001) and these examples are further elaborated by the use of other literature.

2.1 The Case

Copeland and Antikarov (2001) presents a comparative analysis between the three most popular capital budgeting techniques on the basis of a case study. These techniques include the net present value, decision trees and real options. In this case study we could decide to invest right now in a project that will cost \$115 million next year, or to defer until the end of a year. The project cash flows are uncertain and provides a 50–50 probability of either \$170 million or \$65 million. The risk-free rate is the rate of interest that can be earned without assuming any risk. This is the minimum required rate that investors want to earn on their investment. It is important to note that Copeland and Antikarov (2001) presents a risk-free rate of 10 %, but later on use 8 % for their calculations. In the next section we will start with the net present value analysis.

L. Peters, *Real Options Illustrated*, SpringerBriefs in Finance,
DOI 10.1007/978-3-319-28310-4_2

2.2 Net Present Value Analysis

Suppose there is another project that has the same risk characteristics, i.e. the twin security, as the project under consideration. The cash flows of this twin security are perfectly correlated with those of the project and the twin security has a market price of \$20 per share. The cash flows of both projects are shown in Table 2.1.

We will use the contingent claims approach to estimate the NPV of the project by creating a portfolio of securities whose returns exactly replicate the payouts of our project. We can then use the *law of one price*. This states that when there is no arbitrage pricing, i.e. the ruling out of arbitrage opportunities, two assets with the same payoff must have the same market price. In case the two assets are being mispriced relative to each other, an opportunity for arbitrage exists.

We create a replicating portfolio that has exactly the same payouts as our project. This portfolio consists of m shares of the twin security and B risk-free bonds and we have to find the values for m and B. A risk-free bond is a bond that repays interest and principal with absolute certainty. This portfolio has an up and down state payoff and therefore we have two equations from which we can find the two unknowns m and B. And r is the risk-free rate.

$$\textit{Replicating portfolio pay outs in up state}: m \times 34 + B \times (1 + r) = 170 \quad (2.1)$$

$$\textit{Replicating portfolio pay outs in down state}: m \times 13 + B \times (1 + r) = 65 \quad (2.2)$$

To solve the equation we can eliminate the B -variable by subtracting one equation from another.

$$m \times (34 - 13) = 170 - 65$$
$$m = (170 - 65)/(34 - 13) = 5$$

Substitute the value $m = 5$ into Eqs. (2.1) or (2.2) in order to find the value of B. We will illustrate this on the basis of the up state portfolio:

$$\textit{Replicating portfolio pay outs in up state}: 5 \times 34 + B \times (1 + r) = 170$$
$$B = \frac{170 - (5 \times 34)}{1 + 8\ \%} = 0$$

Solving the equation, we find that $m = 5$ and $B = 0$, from these values and the value of the share of the twin security (\$20 million) we can derive the value of the twin security:

Table 2.1 Cash flows of the project and its twin security in million dollars

	Our project	Twin security
Cash flow in up state	\$170	\$34
Cash flow in down state	\$ 65	\$13

$$\textit{Present value of the replicating portfolio}: \quad m \times 20 + B = 5 \times 20 + 0 = \$100 \textit{ million}$$

According to the *law of one price* the value of the project equals \$100 million as well. Since the outlay equals \$115 million in year 1, being discounted back at the risk-free rate we find the present value $\$115/(1 + 8\%) = \$106{,}48$ million. Thus the net present value of the project is:

$$\textit{Net present value of the project} = \$100 - \$106.48 = -\$6.48 \textit{ million}$$

The NPV of this project is negative and therefore we would reject the project. In the next section we will explain how this project is valued according to the decision tree analysis method.

2.3 Decision Tree Analysis

Decision tree analysis (DTA) does an attempt to capture the value of flexibility underlying the investment project. This approach allows to postpone the investment as more information about the project cash flows becomes available over time and then make a decision. This is called a deferral option. The cash payoffs for the right to defer are shown in Table 2.2:

The NPV of the project is calculated by discounting the expected cash flows, given the right to defer, at the weighted average cost of capital (WACC). The WACC is the average cost of capital on the firm's existing projects and activities and the appropriate discount rate to use for cash flows with risk that is similar to that of the overall firm. Objective probabilities,[1] q for the up and $(1 - q)$ for the down movement, are used to determine NPV of the project.

Table 2.2 Cash pay outs for deferral

	Our project	Investment	Net	Defer
Cash flow in up state	\$170	\$115	\$170–\$115 = \$55	max (\$55, \$0) = \$55
Cash flow in down state	\$ 65	\$115	\$65–\$115 = –\$50	max (–\$50, \$0) = \$0

[1] This probability represents a real-world probability measure to obtain the upstate and downstate volatilities. This is in contrast to the risk-neutral probability, which is used for risk-neutral real option-pricing. In case of risk-neutral probabilities, cash flows are adjusted in such a way that these are discounted at the risk-free rate instead of the WACC.

$$Net\ present\ value = \frac{q \times V_{defer\ in\ up\ state} + (1-q) \times V_{defer\ in\ down\ state}}{1 + WACC}$$

We plug the known values $q = (1-q) = 0.5$, $V_{defer\ in\ up\ state} = 55$ and $V_{defer\ in\ down\ state} = 0$, into the previous equation:

$$Net\ present\ value = \frac{0.5 \times 55 + 0.5 \times 0}{1 + WACC} \tag{2.3}$$

We will calculate the WACC on the basis of the twin security that was discussed in the previous section. The current value for a share of the twin security is $20 million, the value in the up and down state are respectively $34 and $13 million. The calculation of the WACC is as follows:

$$V_0 = \frac{q \times V_u + (1-q) \times V_d}{1 + WACC}$$

$$20 = \frac{0.5 \times 34 + (1 - 0.5) \times 13}{1 + WACC}$$

$$WACC = \left[\frac{0.5 \times 34 + (1 - 0.5) \times 13}{20}\right] - 1 = 17.5\%$$

We plug the WACC = 17.5 % into Eq. (2.3) in order to calculate the NPV:

$$\begin{aligned} Net\ present\ value &= \frac{0.5 \times 55 + 0.5 \times 0}{1 + WACC} \\ &= \frac{0.5 \times 55 + 0.5 \times 0}{1 + 17.5\%} \\ &= \$23.40\ million \end{aligned}$$

By incorporating flexibility, i.e. having the right to defer the decision, the NPV of the project has increased from −$6.48 to $23.40 million. Therefore, the value of the deferral option, using the DTA approach is $23.40 − −$6.48 = $29.88 million.

DTA appears to be a plausible approach for solving real options. However, the major concern of the DTA approach is that it violates the *law of one price*. The WACC of 17.5 % is appropriate for a 50–50 chance, and therefore only applicable to 50–50 chance situation, which is not the case of the cash flows of the deferral option Schwartz and Trigeorgis (2001) and Wang and Halala (2010). As illustrated in Table 2.2, the cash flows of the deferral option, i.e. $55 en $0 are not perfectly correlated with the cash flows of the project, $170 and $65. To avoid violation of the *law of one price* by the DTA approach, we need to use real options analysis.

2.4 Real Options Analysis

Copeland and Antikarov (2001) presents two approaches of contingent claims for valuing risky investment projects using real options theory, which will be discussed in this section. The first is the replicating portfolio approach and here we create a replicating portfolio similar to that of the NPV, but its payouts must be the same as those of the deferral option. The second approach is the risk-neutral approach where a hedge portfolio is created to determine the value of the option.

2.4.1 *Replicating Portfolio Approach*

We create a replicating portfolio that is composed of m shares of \$20 million per share and B dollars of the risk-free bond whose present value is \$1 per bond. From this, we can find equations analogous to the Eqs. (2.1) and (2.2) in Sect. 2.2, where the payouts of the replicating portfolio should be equal to the payouts of the deferral option (see Table 2.2). This will result in the following equation:

$$\textit{Replicating portfolio pay outs in up state}: \; m \times 34 + B \times (1 + r) = 55 \tag{2.4}$$

$$\textit{Replicating portfolio pay outs in down state}: \; m \times 13 + B \times (1 + r) = 0 \tag{2.5}$$

And again, to solve the equation we can eliminate the B-variable (Bonds) by subtracting one equation from the other.

$$m \times (34 - 13) = 55 - 0$$

$$m = \frac{55 - 0}{34 - 13} = 2.62$$

Substitute the value $m = 2.62$ into Eqs. (2.4) of (2.5) in order to find the value of B. We will illustrate this on the basis of the up state portfolio:

$$\textit{Replicating portfolio pay outs in up state}: 2.62 \times 34 + B \times (1 + r) = 55$$

$$B = \frac{55 - (2.62 \times 34)}{1 + 8\%} = -31.56$$

Solving the equation, we find that $m = 2.62$ and $B = -31.56$, which implies that we buy 2.62 shares of the twin security and borrow \$31.56 million. From these values, we can derive the value of the replicating portfolio through the price of one share of the twin security (\$20 million):

$$\textit{Present value replicating portfolio} = m \times 20 + B \times 1$$
$$= 2.62 \times 20 - 31.56 \times 1 = \$20.84\,\textit{million}$$

The value of the project is $20.84 million, which is the same as the present value of the replicating portfolio. The value of the flexibility due to the right to defer is $20.84 − − $6.48 = $27.32 million, this in contrast to the obtained value $29.88 using the DTA approach.

2.4.2 Risk-Neutral Probability Approach

The risk-neutral probability approach is the second approach that is discussed by Copeland and Antikarov (2001). We create a hedge-portfolio composed of one share of the underlying risky asset and a short position in m shares of the option that is being priced, in this example a call option with the right to defer. We choose m in a way that the portfolio is risk-free after the first time-period. The hedge portfolio is riskless, because the value of the call option decreases as the value of its underlying risky asset decreases. Since we have taken a short position in a call, and therefore having the right to sell the call option at a predetermined price, our wealth goes up. And in this way, we can offset the decrease of the value of the underlying risky asset by taking a short position in m shares of the option.

Our hedge portfolio is thus composed of one share of the underlying risky asset and m shares of the option. Moreover, the value of our hedge portfolio in the upstate should be equal to the value of our hedge portfolio in the down state and is shown in the following equation:

$$V_u - m \times C_u = V_d - m \times C_d \tag{2.6}$$

where V_u = value underlying risky asset in up state
V_d = value underlying risky asset in down state
C_u = Call option value in up state
C_d = Call option value in down state

In order to find m we rewrite Eq. [2.6] as follows:

$$\begin{aligned} m \times C_u - m \times C_d &= V_u - V_d \\ m \times (C_u - C_d) &= V_u - V_d \\ m &= \frac{V_u - V_d}{C_u - C_d} \end{aligned} \tag{2.7}$$

Look again at Table 2.2, it is shown that the up state value of the underlying risky asset is $170 and the value of the call option is $55. Whereas the down state value of the underlying risky asset is $65 and the value of the call option is $0. Substituting these values into the Eq. [2.7] we obtain:

$$m = \frac{170 - 65}{55 - 0} = \frac{105}{55} = 1.91$$

From this it is shown that the resulting payoff of the hedge portfolio is identical in either the up state and the down state:

$$\textit{Hedge portfolio payoff in the up state}: V_u - m \times C_u = 170 - 1.91 \times 55 = \$65$$

$$\textit{Hedge portfolio payoff in the down state}: V_d - m \times C_d = 65 - 1.91 \times 0 = \$65$$

Knowing how to compose our hedge portfolio, we are able to obtain the value of the call option C_0. Since we have a riskless hedge portfolio, this portfolio will earn the risk-free rate after the first time-period and therefore the resulting payoff will be identical in either the up or the down state. We solve the following equation by using the payout in the up state:

$$(V_0 - m \times C_0) \times (1 + r) = V_u - m \times C_u$$

$$V_0 - m \times C_0 = \frac{V_u - m \times C_u}{1 + r}$$

$$-m \times C_0 = \frac{V_u - m \times C_u}{1 + r} - V_0$$

From this we can obtain C_0:

$$\begin{aligned} C_0 &= \frac{\left[\frac{V_u - m \times C_u}{1 + r} - V_0\right]}{-m} \\ &= \frac{\left[\frac{170 - 1.91 \times 55}{1 + 8\%} - 100\right]}{-1.91} \\ &= \frac{\left[\left(\frac{65}{1.08}\right) - 100\right]}{-1.91} \\ &= -\frac{39.81481}{-1.91} = \$20.84\ \textit{million} \end{aligned} \tag{2.8}$$

And indeed, both risk-neutral valuation and the replicating portfolio approach deliver identical results.

Why is this approach called risk-neutral valuation? We can explain this by combining Eqs. [2.7] and [2.8] with

$$V_u = u \times V_0 \text{ and } V_d = d \times V_0,$$

where

$$u = \text{ up movement } (= 170/100 = 1.7)$$

$$d = \text{down movement } (= 65/100 = 0.65)$$

and consecutively we can derive C_0 as follows:

$$C_0 = \left[C_u \times \left(\frac{(1+r)-d}{u-d}\right) + C_d \times \left(\frac{u-(1+r)}{u-d}\right)\right] + (1+r)$$

Then we define $p = \left(\frac{(1+r)-d}{u-d}\right)$ and $(1-p) = \left(\frac{u-(1+r)}{u-d}\right)$, where p and $(1-p)$ are defined as 'risk-neutral' probabilities. These are the so-called "risk-neutral" probabilities, because the present value of the call option is equal to the expected payouts multiplied by probabilities that adjust them for their risk. Therefore, these cash flows can be discounted at the risk-free rate. The risk-neutral probabilities do not represent "real" probabilities of future events for the up and down state. The "real" probabilities are called the objective probabilities q and $(1-q)$, which were used in the decision tree analysis. The risk-neutral probabilities are constructed in such a way that the adjusted cash flows can be discounted at the risk-free rate. Risk-neutral probabilities are also known as risk-adjusted probabilities or hedging probabilities.

2.5 Evaluation

Traditional discounted cash flow approaches, such as the NPV, cannot properly capture management's flexibility to revise future decisions in response to unexpected developments. Decision tree analysis does an attempt to capture the value of this flexibility underlying the investment project. However, DTA fails to adjust the discount rate in order to account for changes in the risk pattern of a project's cash flows and therefore violates the *law of one price*. Real Options Analysis doesn't have this problem and therefore avoids the violation of the *law of one price*. Copeland and Antikarov (2001) illustrates this on this basis of two equivalent but seemingly different approaches to valuing options: the replicating portfolio approach and the risk-neutral valuation approach.

A well-known drawback of Real Options Analysis using the contingent claims approach is that only in complete markets every contingent claim is perfectly replicable. In practice, however, this is not always the case and then the contingent claims approach for real options cannot be applied. Furthermore, contingent claims is generally based on the no-arbitrage principle, where an arbitrage opportunity is a way of making money with no initial investment without any possibility of loss. Again, this assumption does not always hold.

In this chapter we have presented the NPV, decision tree analysis and Real Options Analysis as separate approaches, however, there is sufficient real options literature, for example by Van Putten and MacMillan (Van Putten and MacMillan 2004), that advocates the integration of both the NPV and Real Options Analysis.

Real Options Analysis provides methods for valuing flexibility with option pricing, which is only a valuable approach when the value of flexibility exceeds the value without flexibility to a great extent. Otherwise we can save us the trouble and use the NPV instead, given the fact that flexibility does not have a substantial impact on the total value. The relevance of real options depends on the relevance of the flexibility for the value. The relevance of flexibility is determined by the following determinants:

- The length of time the project can be deferred. The longer a project can be deferred, in other words the more the maturity date lies in the future, the more valuable an option will be.
- Project risk. Risk is one of the key-drives of project value, because it maximizes the upside potential and minimizes the downside risk. Risk is also called 'volatility' according to the real options terminology. The greater the expected risk or volatility, the higher the option or project value and hence the value of flexibility.
- The level of interest rates. In case of a put option, the higher the interest rates, the higher the discount rates, the lower the present value of the future cash flows and therefore decreases the value of flexibility, i.e. the option value. In case of a call option, higher discount rates result in lower costs to exercise the option, and therefore increases the price of a call option.
- How exclusive the owner's right is to exercise the option. When a firm has the exclusive rights to flexibility, then this is more valuable in comparison to the situation where this exclusive right has to be shared with other firms.

References

Copeland T, Antikarov V (2001) Real options a practitioners guide. TEXERE, New York/London

Schwartz ES, Trigeorgis L (eds) (2001) Real options and investment under uncertainty classical readings and recent contributions. The MIT Press, Cambridge/London

Van Putten AB, MacMillan IC (2004) Making real options really work. Harv Bus Rev 82(12):134

Wang A, Halal W (2010) Comparison of real asset valuation models: a literature review. Int J Bus Manage 5(5):14–24

Chapter 3
Real Options Methods Illustrated

In this chapter we will discuss different approaches to real options pricing. We will start with the analytical solution of the Black-Scholes equation, which will be applied to the case of Netscape. Subsequently, we will present the Cox-Ross-Rubinstein Approach to option pricing, a numerical method for solving dynamic programming problems. Dynamic programming problems are often solved by partial differential equations, which can become very complex and their analytical solutions are even more complex. Therefore, analytical dynamic programming is beyond the scope of this book. But, we will elaborate on numerical dynamic programming using the numerical method of Copeland and Antikarov (2001), which is applied to the case of Portes. This method is a combination of dynamic programming, contingent claims and Monte Carlo simulation. Furthermore, the case of Boeing is used to demonstrate an application of the Monte Carlo simulation approach by Datar and Mathews (2007). We will conclude the discussion on real options approaches with the spreadsheet approach of de Neufville et al. (2006), which includes the use of Monte Carlo simulation in Excel®, and optimizes the decision regarding the design of a parking garage. This final method is more known to the field of engineering, however, it's a very interesting method to use, because it demonstrates the impact and importance of probability distributions on real options value. We will discuss this in more detail in Chap. 4. The concluding part of this chapter is the evaluation of the real options approaches by discussing the pros and cons of each approach.

3.1 Netscape: Black-Scholes

Fisher Black and Myron Scholes are the pioneers for generating a closed-form solution for the price of a European call option. The Black–Scholes model was first published in the 1973 paper *The Pricing of Options and Corporate Liabilities*. Even though the Black-Scholes model was initially developed for financial options,

L. Peters, *Real Options Illustrated*, SpringerBriefs in Finance,
DOI 10.1007/978-3-319-28310-4_3

especially in the early years when real options was not widely applied, the Black-Scholes model served as the economic foundation for real options. Notwithstanding Black-Scholes is limited to providing mere approximations because of the limitations of its key assumptions, it is widely employed as a useful approximation for option pricing. Since Black and Scholes (1973) doesn't provide a practical application of their model to real options, we will use the example by Buckley et al. (2002) to demonstrate the application of Black-Scholes to the context of real options.

3.1.1 The Valuation Formula

Black and Scholes (1973) presents the following equation for valuing a call option w(x, t), i.e. a multivariate function of the stock price x and time t:

$$w(x,t) = xN(d_1) - ce^{r(t-t^*)}N(d_2)$$
$$d_1 = \frac{\ln\left(\frac{x}{c}\right) + \left(r + \frac{1}{2}v^2\right)(t^* - t)}{v\sqrt{t^* - t}} \tag{3.1}$$
$$d_2 = \frac{\ln\left(\frac{x}{c}\right) + \left(r - \frac{1}{2}v^2\right)(t^* - t)}{v\sqrt{t^* - t}}$$

where

- N(d) is the cumulative normal density function
- v^2 is the variance rate of the return on the stock
- c is the exercise price
- x is the stock price
- t* is the maturity date
- t is the current date
- r is the interest rate

As mentioned previously, the Black-Scholes model can only be used under restrictive assumptions. These are the key assumptions underlying the Black-Scholes model as they were formulated by Black and Scholes (1973):[1]

(a) The short-term interest rate is known and is constant through time.
(b) The stock price follows a random walk in continuous time with a variance rate proportional to the square of the stock price. Thus the distribution of possible

[1] We present the exact formulation of the key assumptions as were defined by Black and Scholes in 1973. In the real options literature, these assumptions have been described differently by different authors, such as Copeland and Antikarov (2001a) and Hull (2009a).

stock prices at the end of any finite interval is log- normal. The variance rate of the return on the stock is constant.

(c) The stock pays no dividends or other distributions.
(d) The option is "European," that is, it can only be exercised at maturity.
(e) There are no transaction costs in buying or selling the stock or the option.
(f) It is possible to borrow any fraction of the price of a security to buy it or to hold it, at the short-term interest rate.
(g) There are no penalties to short selling. A seller who does not own a security will simply accept the price of the security from a buyer, and will agree to settle with the buyer on some future date by paying him an amount equal to the price of the security on that date.

Because of these restrictive assumptions, Black and Scholes (1973) is able to derive a closed-form solution for the price of a European call based on the properties of a hedged position. We will not go into any further details of this. However, this will become more clear when we discuss the method by Cox et al. (1979). Assumption (b) describes that the stock price follows a random walk in continuous time, i.e. the stock price follows a special type of stochastic process known as geometric Brownian motion. Since this property plays a key role in real options analysis, we will take a closer look at this property in the next section.

3.1.1.1 Geometric Brownian Motion

A Brownian motion, also known as a Wiener process, has been used in physics to describe the motion of a particle, and in finance and economics it has been used to describe the stochastic process (volatility) of stock prices. A variable z follows a Wiener process if it has the following two properties:

- Property 1. The change dz during a small interval of dt is $dz = \varepsilon\sqrt{dt}$, where ε is a random drawing from a standard normal distribution $\phi(0, 1)$
- Property 2. The values of dz for any two different short intervals of time dt are independent

The standard normal distribution is often used in probability theory and is a normal distribution with a mean of 0 and standard deviation of 1. The probability density function is shown in Fig. 3.1. Two well-known properties of the normal distribution are:

- About 68 % of its values lie within one standard distribution of its mean. To find this range, take the value of the standard deviation, then find the mean plus this amount, and the mean minus this amount: $[\mu - \sigma, \mu + \sigma]$.
- About 95 % of its values lie within two standard deviations of the mean. To find this range take 2 times the standard deviation, then add it to and subtract it from the mean: $[\mu - 2\sigma, \mu + 2\sigma]$.

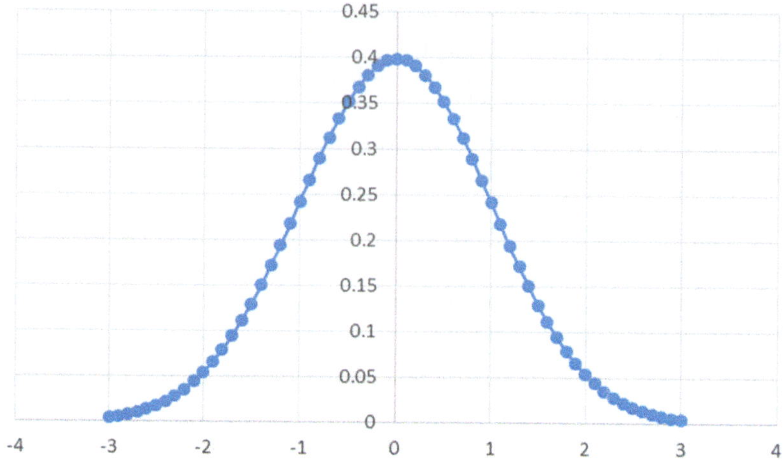

Fig. 3.1 Standard normal distribution

The second property of the Wiener process, i.e. that the values of two short intervals of dt are independent, implies that z follows a Markov process. This means that only the current value is relevant and is independent of its historic values, and therefore can be thought of as 'memoryless'. This is a frequently made assumption for stock prices and is consistent with the 'weak form of market efficiency'. This means that the present price of a stock impounds all the information contained in a record of past prices (Hull 2009a). The Markov property implies that only the current stock price is relevant for predicting future prices and that the stock price of last month, week or day is irrelevant. However, in practice we intuitively expect that a rise in yesterday's stock price would lead to an increase of tomorrow's stock price as well. The Markov property denies this relation and this may sound somewhat counter-intuitive. In other words, according to the Markov property there is no need to have a look at the figures of the stock exchange, since they do not provide us any information of the current stock prices changes.

The question is how to obtain the Wiener process. Suppose that the value z of a variable that follows a Wiener process is initially zero, $z(0)$. The value of z at the next time interval dt is determined as follows:

1. Draw ε from a standard normal distribution
2. Calculate $\sqrt{dt}$
3. Find dz, the change of z, by multiplying ε and $\sqrt{dt}$
4. Add dz to the previous value of z to acquire the new value of z

Since we have found the value of $z(0 + dt)$, we are able repeat the same procedure and find all possible values of $z(t)$.

We will illustrate the above-mentioned procedure with the following example. Our Wiener process has an initial value of $z(0) = 25$ and a time interval of length

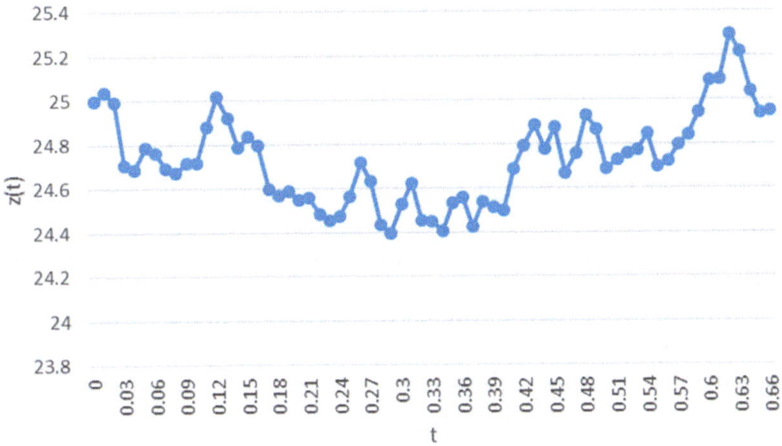

Fig. 3.2 Example of Wiener process

$dt = 0.01$. We will follow the same procedure as before in order to find the value of $z(0.01)$.

1. We perform a random drawing, ε, from a standard normal distribution and we get $\varepsilon = -0.35$.
2. $\sqrt{dt} = 0.1$
3. $dz = \varepsilon \times \sqrt{dt} = -0.35 \ \times 0.1 = \ -0.035$
4. The value after $dt = 0.01$ becomes $z(0) + -0.035 = 25 + -0.035 = 24.965$. We will find that $z(0.01) = 24.965$.

A Wiener process $z(t)$ is illustrated in Fig. 3.2 and we can recognize the stochastic process of the stock price in this figure.

A generalized Wiener process $x(t)$ uses the basic Wiener process z to add noise or variability to the (linear) path followed by x, the drift. We define the change of x in terms of the change of z as follows:

$$dx \ = \ adt \ + \ bdz,$$

with a and b defined as constants.

The adt term represents the drift rate and the bdz represents the noise or variability. Notice that we still use the standard normal distribution for z. In other words, a generalized Wiener process is a combination of a linear trend line and noise. Parameter a represents the slope of the linear trend line and parameter b can be regarded as the amplifier of the noise, which is caused by the Wiener process z.

How do we obtain the generalized Wiener process? Suppose that x follows a generalized Wiener process with an initial value of $x(0)$ and that the parameters a and b are known. The value of x at the next time interval of dt is obtained as follows:

1. Draw ε from a standard normal distribution
2. Calculate $\sqrt{dt}$

3. Find dz, the change of z, by multiplying ε and $\sqrt{dt}$
4. Multiply dz with the parameter b to find $b \times dz$
5. Multiply dt with the parameter a to find $a \times dt$
6. Add $a \times dt$ to $b \times dz$ to find dx, which is the change of x
7. Add dx to the previous value of x to acquire our new value of x

Since we have found the value of $z(0 + dt)$, we are able to repeat the same procedure and find all possible values of $x(t)$. When referring back to the previous procedure, we notice that the 'noise' component is calculated in step 4 and the 'drift' component in step 5.

We will illustrate the above-mentioned procedure with the following example. Our generalized Wiener process of x with parameters $a = 5$ and $b = 1$, an initial value of $x(0) = 0$ and a time interval of length, $dt = 0.01$. We will follow the same procedure as before in order to find the value of $z(0.01)$.

1. We draw ε from a standard normal distribution and we get $\varepsilon = -0.35$
2. $\sqrt{dt} = 0.1$
3. $dz = \varepsilon \times \sqrt{dt} = -0.35 \times 0.1 = -0.035$.
4. $b \times dz = 1 \times -0.035 = -0.035$
5. $a \times dt = 5 \times 0.01 = 0.05$
6. $dx = adt + bdz = 0.05 + -0.035 = 0.015$.
7. The value of x at time $t = 0.01$ becomes $x(0) + -0.015 = 0 + 0.015 = 0.015$, i.e. $x(0.01) = 0.015$.

In Fig. 3.3 a generalized Wiener process is represented by the gray line, the orange line indicates the drift, whereas the noise is represented by the blue line because of its underlying Wiener process.

We can make a further generalization of the generalized Wiener process where the parameters *a and b* are functions, instead of constant parameters, of the underlying variables x and t. Algebraically, an Itô process can be written as:

$$dx = a(x, t)dt + b(x, t)dz$$

We will model the stock price S as an Itô process and we take $a(S, t) = \mu S$ en $b(S, t) = \sigma S$. This results in a geometric Brownian motion:

$$dS = \mu Sdt + \sigma Sdz$$

μ represents the expected rate of return and σ represents the volatility of stock price S. The most widely used model for stochastic modelling of stock price (indices) in continuous time is the Geometric Brownian motion.

The next question we can ask ourselves is how to obtain the parameter values of μ and σ. In Hull (2009b) we can read that the value of an option does depend on σ of the underlying value, but does not depend on μ. When we look back at Eq. (3.1), it is shown that σ represents a parameter value, whereas μ is not. Therefore, we do not have to worry about the parameter value for μ of the underlying value.

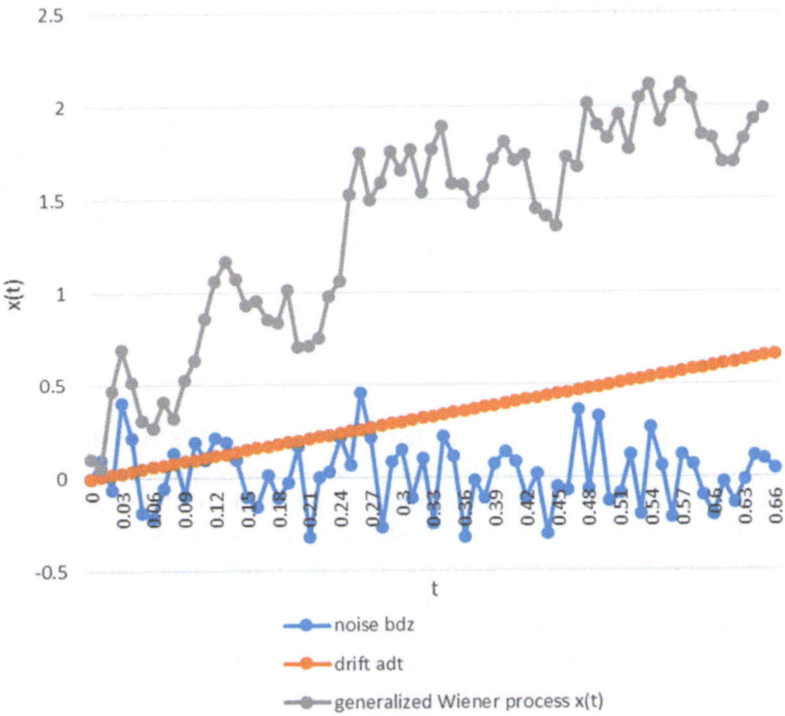

Fig. 3.3 Example of generalized Wiener process with $a = 5$ and $b = 1$ including drift and Wiener process

An estimation method for the parameter value σ of has been described by Hull (2009c). Copeland and Antikarov (2001a) uses Monte Carlo simulation to obtain the parameter value of σ, which will be discussed later in this book.

The final, but essential question is how do we know whether or not a specific process is geometric Brownian motion. To answer this question we return to the two properties of a Wiener process:

- Property 1. The change dz during a small interval of dt is $dz = \varepsilon\sqrt{dt}$, where ε is a random drawing from a standardized normal distribution $\phi(0, 1)$
- Property 2. The values of dz for any two different short intervals of time dt are independent

A process can only be regarded as a geometric Brownian motion if the two properties are true for this given process. This could be verified on the basis of historical data. We will not further explain this topic and for further reading on concrete validation of the geometric Brownian motion we refer to Yen and Yen (1999) and Marathe and Ryan (2005).

3.1.2 *The Main Objective*

When Black and Scholes published their famous Black and Scholes model (3.1) in 1973, other option pricing models had been circulating as well at that time. However, each of these models faced their drawbacks and therefore were not applicable. For example the parameters for some of these models could not be identified. Black and Scholes were able to find a closed form solution, under restrictive assumptions, for the price of European call.

3.1.3 *The Case: Netscape*

In 1995 Netscape issued 5 million shares publicly for \$28 per share. Buckley et al. (2002) shows how to obtain this value by using the Black and Scholes equation. Even though, the parameter values required for deriving the price of \$28 per share are very unlikely, we can still use their methodology to illustrate the Black and Scholes equation. Buckley et al. (2002) breaks the total value of one share of Netscape into two components, a base-case and real options. Discounted cash flow analysis is used to model the base case and this results in base case value per share of over \$15. Thereafter, the parameters from Table 3.1 are used to obtain the value of the real options component and we interpret 'the value per share of over \$15', as \$15.4.

When we insert these parameter values into the Black and Scholes equation (3.1), for example by using Excel © with the values of $d_1 = 1.23$ and $d_2 = -1.45$, we obtain \$12.3 per share for the real options component. The total value of a Netscape share is indeed \$15.4 + \$12.3 = \$28 per share.

3.1.4 *Strengths and Weaknesses*

The Black and Scholes Option Pricing model (3.1) is the most widely used model to value options. A closed form solution (insert the parameter values into the equation and the result is produced right away) is more straightforward and therefore easier

Table 3.1 Parameters for Black-Scholes formula to value Netscape shares

Symbol	Meaning	Value
V^2	Variance of the return on the stock	0.36
c	Exercise price	81
x	Stock price	15.4
t*	Maturity date	20
t	Current date	0
t* – t	Time to expiration	20
r	Interest rate	0.07

to understand than the complex real options methods that contain stochastic calculus. However, a closed form solution for the Black and Scholes equation can only be applied when it relies on its seven strict assumptions. These assumptions do not hold in the real world. Especially, the assumption that the stock price follows a geometric Brownian motion is regarded as a serious draw back in real options analysis. Another limitation of Black and Scholes is that it is not well suited to valuing compound options, and is better suited for simple options. Moreover, the Black and Scholes model allows for only one source of risk or volatility. Knowing the shortcomings of the Black and Scholes model and therefore its repercussions of applying the model to the real world, Black and Scholes is widely employed as a useful approximation for option pricing. Furthermore, the derivation of the Black and Scholes equation requires advanced mathematics, such as Itô-calculus, which complicates the accessibility of this approach. Nevertheless, Black and Scholes is widely used in practice as a useful approximation to check the validity of more refined real options models.

3.2 Option Pricing: Cox, Ross and Rubinstein

Cox et al. (1979) (CRR) presents a simple discrete-time model using the contingent claims approach following a numerical procedure for valuing options. This binomial lattice approach forms the basis for many numerical methods that are present nowadays. The CRR method as well as Black-Scholes were initially developed for valuing financial options and later on were introduced to real options. Since the CRR method is one of the foundations of real options, we will discuss this method in detail here. We will first explain the basic idea underlying the binomial tree method and then will demonstrate the CRR method based on the derivation of the binomial option pricing equation. In the final part of this section we will show how Copeland and Antikarov (2001b) incorporates the CRR-method into their real options approach. At the same time this final part serves as an introduction to the next section about the method of Copeland and Antikarov.

3.2.1 The Basic Idea

In order to illustrate the underlying thought behind the binomial tree method we will use the example of Cox et al. (1979). Suppose the current price of the option is \$50 and at the end of the period the price will be either \$25 of \$100, which is denoted by S^*. The situation is illustrated in Fig. 3.4. After the first time period, the binomial tree presents two possible outcomes for the stock price. A multi-step binomial tree represents a decision tree with multiple possible outcomes for the stock price. Since at each node there are two possible outcomes, this is referred to as a binomial tree.

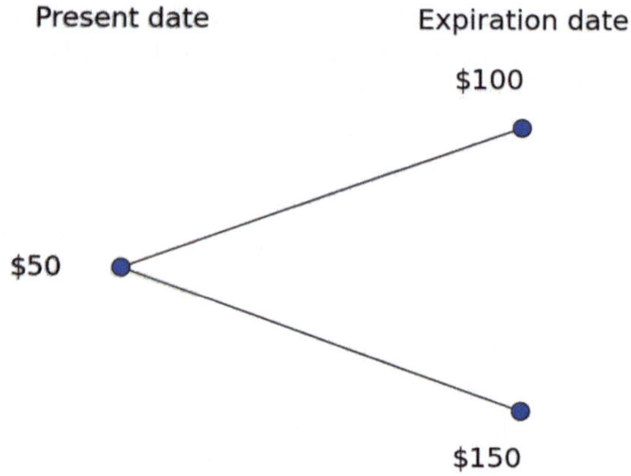

Fig. 3.4 Binomial tree of stock price

At the end of the period we have a call option available, which has a strike price of $K = \$50$ per share. The share pays no dividends and there are no transaction costs, margin requirements and taxes. It is possible to borrow money at an interest rate of 25 % and we can repay the loan at the end of the period. The question is: What is the value of the call option?

We can set up the following riskless portfolio:

1. Write 3 calls
2. Buy shares at $50 each
3. Borrow $40 at 25 % to be paid back at the end of the period.

This is called a levered hedge, since the hedge exactly breaks even at the end of the life of the option no matter which way the price of a share will move. If the share price decreases to $S^* = \$25$, the call option is worthless to the owners of the call, as nobody will buy a share at more than its market price, i.e. where $K = \$50$ whereas the market price is $25. The current value of our shares is $2 \times \$25 = \$50$ and we have a debt of $50, because we have borrowed $40 at an interest rate of 25 %. The total value of our hedge portfolio equals $\$0 + \$50 - \$50 = \$0$. If the share price increases to $S^* = 100$, then the call options will most likely be exercised at a cost of $3 \times (\$100 - \$50) = \$150$. The value of our shares is $2 \times \$100 = \$200$ and our loan at the bank equals $50. Therefore the value of our hedge portfolio is $-\$150 + \$200 - \$50 = \$0$. This is illustrated in Table 3.2.

In order to prevent any arbitrage opportunities from even arising in the first place, the current value of our hedge portfolio has to be equal to the value of this portfolio at the end of the period, in other words has to be zero. From this we can obtain the value of the call option, **C**:

$$3 \times C - 100 + 40 = 0$$
$$C = (100 - 40)/3 = \$20$$

Table 3.2 Value of riskless hedge

	Present date	Expiration date	
		S* = $25	S* = $100
Value of writing 3 calls	3 × C	$0	−$150
Value of buying 2 shares	−$100	$50	$200
Value of borrow $40	$40	−$50	−$50
Total value		$0	$0

From this we can conclude that it's possible to create a portfolio in such a way that the value of the portfolio remains unchanged, regardless of whether the stock price moves up or down. In this way we can determine the value of the call. In order to do so, we only need the strike price K, the underlying stock price S, the up and down movement of the stock price and the interest rate. What is most notable here, is that we do not need to know the probability of a stock going up or down.

This is because the value of the call option entirely depends on the underlying stock price. And indeed, this is an example of the contingent claims approach, of course, under the condition that the option completely depends on the stock price. If this is not the case, the CRR-method cannot be applied. We can also view this example from the perspective of no-arbitrage and because of the existence of no-arbitrage, the value of the call is as it is supposed to be.

Cox et al. (1979) translates the above-mentioned basic idea to a binomial options pricing model to value financial options. The binomial tree can be modified to accommodate for a closed-form solution, which is the binomial option pricing formula. In the next section it is explained how the binomial option pricing formula is derived. We will see that this formula does not always apply, but we can still use the underlying binomial tree method. This will be demonstrated using the example of Copeland and Antikarov (2001b).

3.2.2 *The Binomial Option Pricing Formula*

In the previous section Cox et al. (1979) described the process of a closed-form solution for the valuation of financial options, from a binomial tree to the binomial option pricing model. We assume that the stock price S follows a multiplicative binomial process over discrete periods. Binomial means that a stock price has two possible outcomes: it can go up or go down. A multiplicative process is a process where an increase directly followed by a decrease in the stock price produces the same value as in the situation where a stock price first moves down and after that immediately moves up. The stock price goes up by a factor u with probability q and then goes down by a factor d with probability $(1 - q)$ as is illustrated in Fig. 3.5 for one time period.

We also assume that the interest rate r is constant $(r = 1 + \textit{riskless interest rate})$. Everyone has the opportunity to borrow or lend

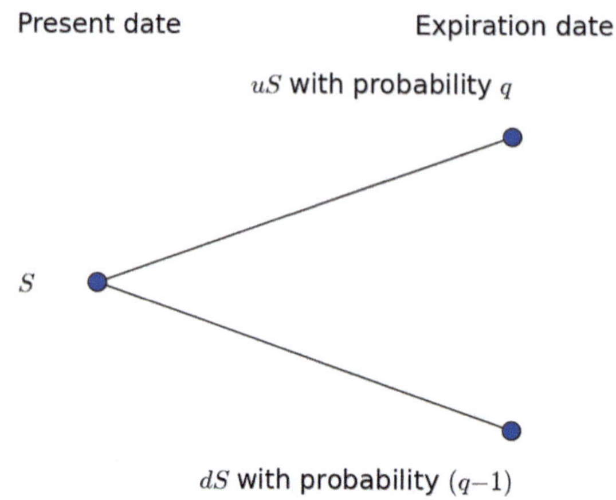

Fig. 3.5 Stock price – one period

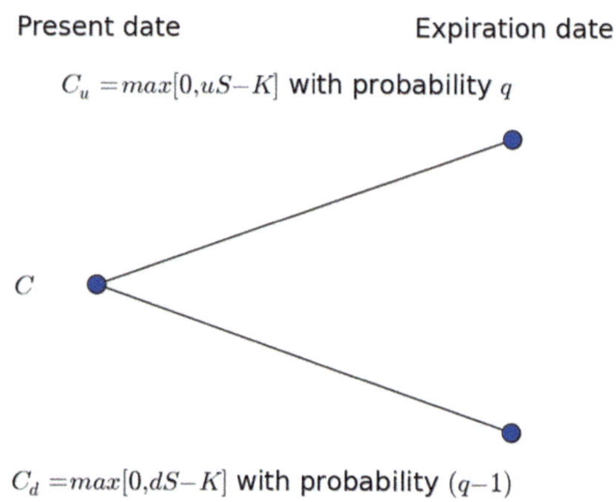

Fig. 3.6 Value call option – one period

as much as they wish at this rate. Again, we will continue to assume there are no taxes, transaction costs and margin requirements. Therefore, we can write as many calls as we can and receive full use of the proceeds. Note, we must have $d < r < u$ to avoid arbitrage opportunities.

Now we are able to derive the value of a European call written on this stock and having in mind that the expiration date is just one period in away. C_u is the value of the call option if the stock goes up and C_d if the stock goes down. A call option only has intrinsic value if the stock price S exceeds the strike price K. If the strike price K is greater than the stock price S, then owners of the call will rather buy the stock on the market than pay its strike price K. This is illustrated in Fig. 3.6.

Considering a portfolio of m shares of stock and B bonds of \$1. The portfolio will cost $m \times S + B$. At the end of the first time-period, the value of the bond is $r \times B$. If the price goes up to $u \times S$, the value of our portfolio equals $m \times u \times S + r \times B$, whereas if the price goes down to $d \times S$, the value of our portfolio will be $m \times d \times S + r \times B$ (Fig. 3.7).

Fig. 3.7 Value portfolio – one period

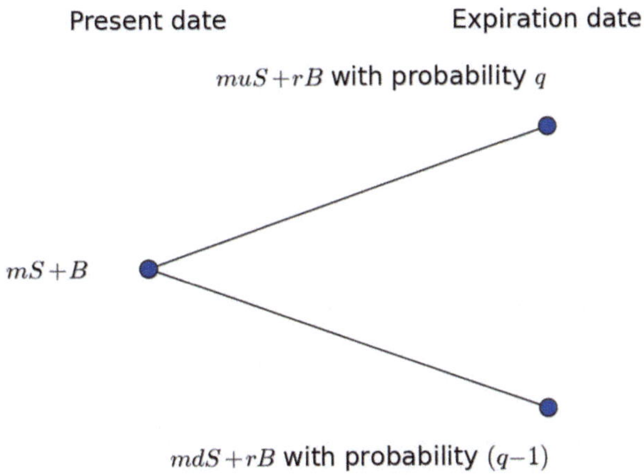

In order to create a hedge portfolio, we will have to define our m and B in such a way that the value of the portfolio in the up and down state at the expiration date is equal to the value of the call. This means:

$$m \times u \times S + r \times B = C_u \tag{3.2}$$

$$m \times d \times S + r \times B = C_d \tag{3.3}$$

Solving these equations we can find m and B. We subtract Eq. (3.3) from (3.2) and we get:

$$m \times u \times S - m \times d \times S = C_u - C_d$$

And with

$$m \times (u \times S - d \times S) = C_u - C_d$$

it follows that

$$m = \frac{C_u - C_d}{(u \times S - d \times S)} = \frac{C_u - C_d}{(u - d) \times S} \tag{3.4}$$

In order to find the correct value for B we can plug this value into Eq. (3.2) or (3.3). We will use Eq. (3.2) and get:

$$\frac{C_u - C_d}{(u - d) \times S} \times u \times S + r \times B = C_u \tag{3.5}$$

We can now rewrite Eq. (3.5) in order to obtain the expression for B:

$$\begin{aligned} \frac{C_u - C_d}{u - d} \times u + r \times B &= C_u \\ B &= \frac{C_d \times u - C_u \times d}{r \times (u - d)} \end{aligned} \tag{3.6}$$

In order to avoid arbitrage opportunities, the value of our portfolio has to be equal to the value of the call option:[2]

$$C = m \times S + B \tag{3.7}$$

We can now insert Eqs. (3.4) for m and (3.6) for B into Eq. (3.7) in order to calculate value of the call option C.

$$\begin{aligned} C &= \frac{C_u - C_d}{(u - d) \times S} \times S + \frac{C_d \times u - C_u \times d}{r \times (u - d)} \\ &= \left[\frac{(r - d)}{(u - d)} \times C_u + \frac{(u - r)}{(u - d)} \times C_d\right] / r \end{aligned}$$

We can rewrite this equation with $p = \frac{r-d}{u-d}$ and $1 - p = \frac{u-r}{u-d}$ as follows:

$$C = [p \times C_u + (1 - p) \times C_d] / r \tag{3.8}$$

Equation (3.8) presents the value of the call option for a one period case. The probability q for the up and down movement of the stock price does not appear in (3.8). The only variables that do appear are the variables S, K, u, d and r. Note that S and K are 'hidden' in C_u and C_d. Moreover, the price of the option does not depend on the investors' attitudes toward risk, since we obtain the same result whether investors are risk-averse or risk-preferring. Finally, we can see that the stock price is the only random variable on which the call value depends on, which is the stock price itself. The derivation of these properties can be explained because the value of the call completely depends on S, K, u, d and r. In other words, we analyze this option in accordance with the contingent claims approach.

We can extend the analysis to a two-step binomial tree. Since the variables u and u are held constant, stock price S follows the path that is presented in Fig. 3.8. Since the stock price follows a multiplicative binomial process, we say the tree is recombining and therefore we have three instead of four end nodes after the second time-period. This is because an up movement followed by a down movement equals a down movement followed by an up movement. This in order to keep the number of nodes and computation time within reasonable limits.

[2] This equation holds, because we are dealing here with a European call option. In case of an American option, this equation only holds if $mS + B > S - K$. Otherwise this is $C = S - K$.

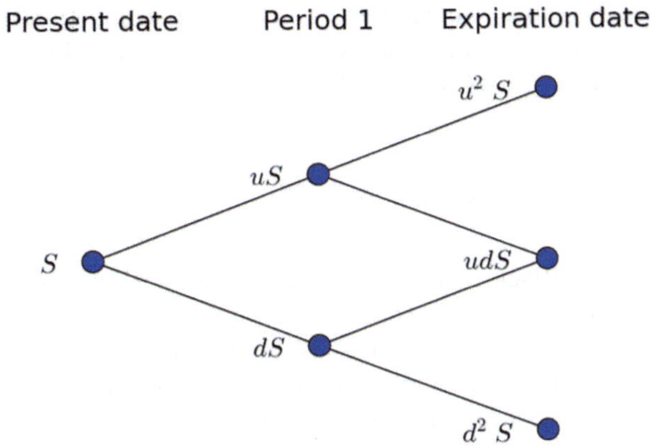

Fig. 3.8 Stock price – two periods

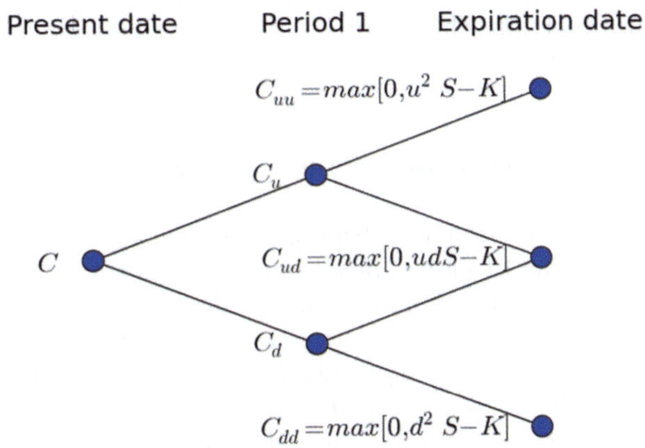

Fig. 3.9 Value call option – two periods

In Fig. 3.9 we can find the call option values in a two-step tree.

If we start at the end nodes and working back through the binomial tree, we can derive the equations for C_u and C_d, which is analogous to (3.8):

$$C_u = [p \times C_{uu} + (1 - p) \times C_{ud}]/r \tag{3.9}$$

$$C_d = [p \times C_{ud} + (1 - p) \times C_{dd}]/r \tag{3.10}$$

Substituting Eqs. (3.9) and (3.10) into (3.8) and note that $C_{ud} = C_{du}$, we get Eq. (3.11):

$$\begin{aligned} C = \big[& p^2 \times \max[0, u^2 \times S - K] \\ & +2 \times p \times (1 - p) \times \max[0, u \times d \times S - K] \\ & + (1 - p)^2 \times \max\left[0, d^2 \times S - K\right] \big]/r^2 \end{aligned} \tag{3.11}$$

We have seen that it's pretty straight-forward to extend Eq. (3.8) to a two-step binomial tree. In addition, all the properties of (3.8) still hold in Eq. (3.11). Using mathematics, we can transform (3.8) to an equation that is analogous to (3.11) for n-period binomial models, which is also referred to as the binomial option pricing formula of Cox, Ross and Rubinstein.

$$C = \left[\sum_{j=0}^{n} \left(\frac{n!}{j!(n-j)!} \right) \times p^j \times (1-p)^{n-j} \times \max\left[0, u^j \times d^{n-j} \times S - K\right] \right] / r^n$$

Unlike Black-Scholes, the binomial option pricing model, a numerical technique, has no closed-form solution for the valuation of financial options. This equation is not used to price real options, because it does not incorporate the possibility for a decision maker whether or not to exercise the option at any time until the expiry moment. However, the underlying binomial tree method is used in real options, where the process followed by the underlying value is modeled as a multiplicative binomial process. Working backward through the tree enables the decision makers to decide on whether or not to exercise the option at any time until the expiry moment.

3.2.2.1 Geometric Brownian Motion

One of the differences between Black and Scholes (1973) and Cox et al. (1979) is that in the Black and Scholes model time is a continuous variable, whereas Cox, Ross and Rubinstein treat time as a discrete variable. In order for the Cox, Ross and Rubinstein model to converge to a continuous-time model, smaller time steps are required as well as an increase in the number of time periods. However, when we multiply the stock price at each node of the binomial tree with the same constant u or d, a problem arises, since the stock price could increase rapidly. For example, suppose that $C = 10$ and $u = 1.1$ and the length of one time interval is 1 s. The maximum stock price after 1 min is equal to $1.1^{60} \times 10 = 3044.8$. This is unrealistic and undesirable.

In order to make sure that the modeled stock price at each node of the binomial tree doesn't fluctuate too much and to preserve the expected standard deviation σ and mean μ of the rate of return of the actual continuous[3] stock price for each time interval, Cox et al. (1979) has derived $u = e^{\sigma\sqrt{h}}$ and $u = 1/d$ for the binomial tree model, where h is the elapsed time between successive stock price changes. This is possible, since the stock price follows a multiplicative binomial process over discrete periods. In other words, the actual, continuous stock price follows a random walk.

[3] A continuous process is one where the price movements of a stock show small constant changes and we are able to follow these changes without having to remove the pen from the paper. In contrast to this, a jump process where stock price movements are discrete, i.e. discrete movements called jumps. Here the stock price can change only at certain fixed points in time.

3.2.3 *The Main Objectives*

Cox et al. (1979) proposes the binomial option pricing model as an alternative to the Black and Scholes model. The derivation of the Black and Scholes model involves advanced mathematics, which is not required for the method of Cox, Ross and Rubinstein. Moreover, Cox, Ross and Rubinstein demonstrate the underlying concepts of arbitrage, contingent claims and dynamic programming. Finally, the founders of the binomial option pricing model have developed an efficient model, since it contains a multiplicative binomial process that limits the number of nodes involved in the tree.

3.2.4 *Strengths and Weaknesses*

The binomial option pricing model of Cox, Ross and Rubinstein has been praised because it made the theory of option pricing accessible to everyone with a limited mathematical background. An advantage in comparison to the Black and Scholes method is that the CRR-method is applicable to both European and American options. A limitation of both aforementioned option pricing models is that the stock price follows the geometric Brownian motion. Even though the binomial trees are recombining, the number of nodes and therefore the computation time could rise significantly if the number of time periods are increased.

3.2.5 *The Binomial Tree Method Illustrated*

We have seen in Sect. 3.2.2 that we are not able to use the binomial option pricing formula of Cox et al. (1979) in the context of real options, but we can use the underlying binomial tree method. In this section we will demonstrate how to apply the binomial tree method using the example of Copeland and Antikarov (2001b). In the next section we will discuss the entire real options approach of Copeland and Antikarov (2001b), and will demonstrate that the binomial tree method is part of this approach.

3.2.5.1 The Case

In this example we derive a method for valuing puts, in this case an abandonment option. A put option gives the buyer of the option the right, but not the obligation, to sell a risky asset at a future date at a predetermined price within a specified period of time. The abandonment option refers to the sales of the asset at any moment for the price of $900. The present value of the asset without flexibility equals $1,000. The up and down movements of the present value are respectively $u = 1.06184$, and $d = 1/u = 0.94176$ and we will analyze four periods, i.e. a period of 4 × quarter = 1 year. The project pays no dividends. The annual risk free rate is 5 % and the *WACC k* is 15 %. The maturity date of the abandonment option is 6 months, i.e. after two time-periods.

3.2.5.2 Event Tree

Figure 3.10 shows a recombining binomial tree, which is based on the present value of the project and the *u* and *d*, for the first half of the year. The event tree of the value of the project is represented by nodes A t/m F. At the end of the first period, the present value in the up state is $1{,}000 \times u = 1{,}000 \times 1.06184 = 1{,}061.84$. This situation is illustrated in Fig. 3.10.

3.2.5.3 Decision Tree

Now we can calculate the option valuation lattice by adding the option to abandon to the event tree of the underlying asset. This will result in a decision tree and at each node (A t/m F) we have to take one of the following decisions:

- The decision to abandon the project (abandonment option)
- The decision to continue with the existing operations without abandoning (profit-maximizing decision)

The decision tree comprises both the value of the project as the underlying asset and the abandonment option. In other words, the current value of the project at a given moment includes the value of the option to abandon. The value of the project including the abandonment option at time t = 0 and t = 1 are not known yet, since

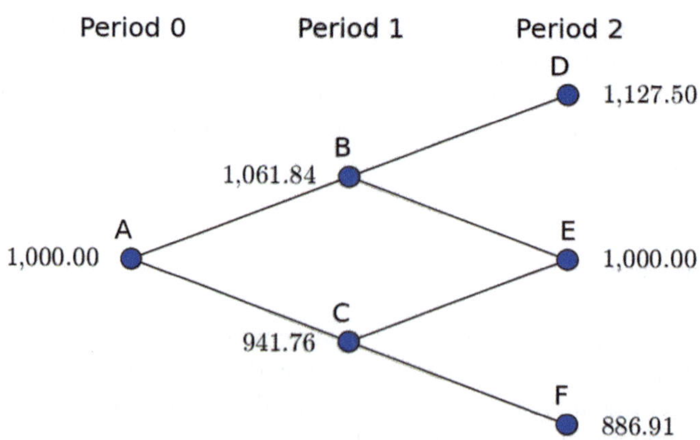

Fig. 3.10 Event tree of value of the project

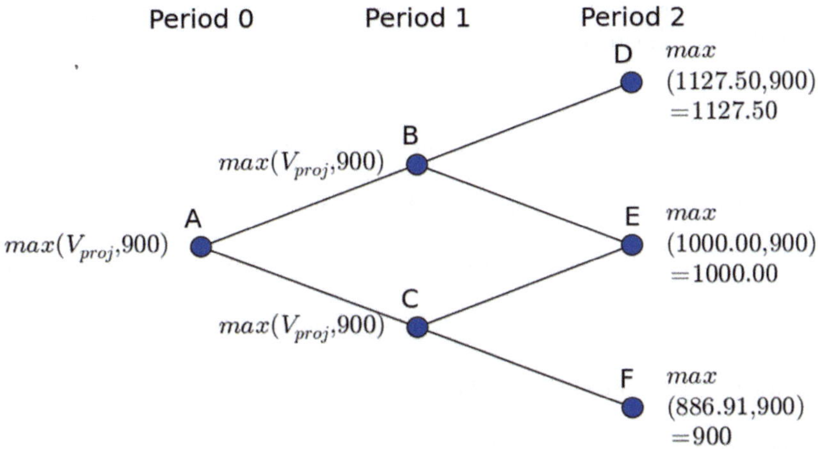

Fig. 3.11 Decision tree of value of the project including abandonment option (only last period)

we first have to figure out whether or not we will exercise the option at time t = 2 and the effect of this decision. Therefore, we will start with the nodes at t =2, because the payoffs of the project for this time interval are known. At node F, the value of the project is \$886.91, whereas the value of the abandonment option is \$900. This is shown in Fig. 3.11. In this case the profit-maximizing decision is to exercise the abandonment option, since *max* (900, 886.91) = 900. We'll perform this procure for each node at time t = 2 and from this we'll obtain the decision tree as is shown in Fig. 3.11. The values at time t = 0 and t = 1 are still unknown.

3.2.5.4 Backward Induction

The next step is to determine the values of the project including the abandonment option at time t = 1 based on the values of the project including the abandonment option at time t = 2 using a process called *backward induction*. The same procedure is repeated for the calculation of the value of the project including the abandonment option at time t = 0 and from this we have obtained the real options value of the project.

For the calculation of project value at node C, but without including the abandonment option for this node, we need to determine the values of the project including the abandonment option at node E and F first. The value at node E (up-state) \$1,000 and at node F (down-state) is \$900.

From here we are able to create a replicating portfolio, where Copeland and Antikarov (2001b) selects the project without flexibility as the underlying asset, which is illustrated in Fig. 3.10. We create a replicating portfolio consisting of *m* shares of the project itself and *B* bonds, so that the value of the replicating portfolio is equal to the value of the project at node C. It turns out from Fig. 3.10

that the value of the project without flexibility at node C is \$941.76, and this results in the following equation:

$$\textit{Replicating portfolio}: \quad m \times 941.76 + B = V_C, \textit{ where}$$
$$V_C = \textit{value project in state C incl abandonment option in period } 2$$

Knowing the values at node E and node F, we get

$$\textit{State E}: \quad m \times u \times 941.76 + (1 + r) \times B = 1{,}000 \tag{3.12}$$

$$\textit{State F}: \quad m \times d \times 941.76 + (1 + r) \times B = 900 \tag{3.13}$$

By subtracting one equation from the other we get:

$$m \times 941.76 \times (u - d) = 1{,}000 - 900$$
$$m = \frac{1{,}000 - 900}{941.76 \times (u - d)}$$
$$= \frac{1{,}000 - 900}{941.76 \times (1.06184 - 0.94176)}$$
$$= \frac{100}{113.09} = 0.8843$$

In order to find the value for B we plug these values into one of the Eqs. (3.12) or (3.13). From Eq. (3.12) of node E, it follows that:

$$\text{State E}: \quad m \times u \times 41.76 + (1 + r) \times B = 1{,}000$$

$$\begin{aligned} B &= \frac{1{,}000 - m \times u \times 941.76}{1 + r} \\ &= \frac{1{,}000 - 0.8843 \times 1.06184 \times 941.76}{1 + r} \end{aligned} \tag{3.14}$$

The annual risk free rate is 5 %. Considering a time-period of 3 months, the value of r will be $5\%/4 = 1.25\%$. By contrast, Copeland and Antikarov (2001b) uses a different risk free rate that is equal to $r = 0.01258$. They do not provide any explanation for the choice of this risk free rate. Anyway, we will use the same risk free rate as them and will plug it into Eq. (3.14):

$$B = \frac{1{,}000 - 0.8843 \times 1.06184 \times 941.76}{1 + 0.01258}$$
$$= \frac{115.70}{1.01258} = 114.27$$

The value of the project at node C is then (knowing that we will make the right decision on whether or not to exercise the abandonment option):

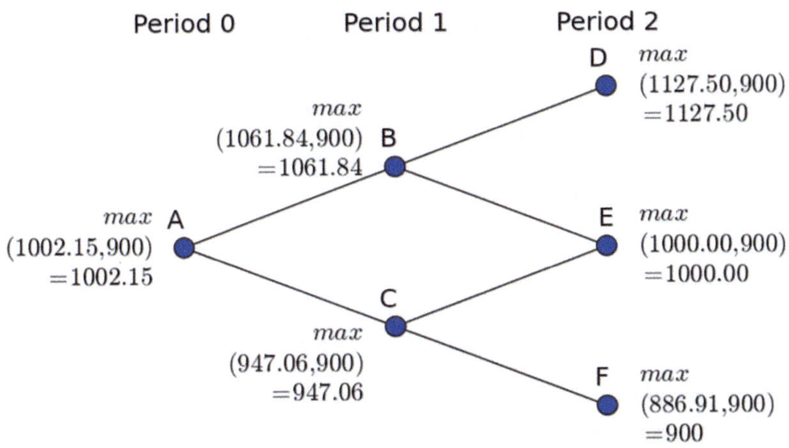

Fig. 3.12 Decision tree of value of the project including abandonment option (all periods)

$$\begin{aligned} V_C &= m \times 941.76 + B \\ &= 0.8843 \times 941.76 + 114.27 = 947.06 \end{aligned}$$

In node C, the value of continuation is higher than the value of the abandonment option and therefore we decide not to exercise the abandonment option at node C.

In a similar way we are able to calculate the value of the project that includes future flexibility for node B and subsequently we will apply the same method to obtain the value for node A. This procedure is illustrated in Fig. 3.12.

3.2.5.5 Value of the Abandonment Option

The value of the project including the abandonment option is equal to the value at node A, which is equal to \$1,002.15. Since the present value of the project, i.e. without the abandonment option, was \$1,000, and therefore the value of the abandonment option is equal to \$1,002.15 − \$1,000 = \$2.15.

In this example we have seen that both Copeland and Antikarov (2001b) and Cox et al. (1979) use a process called backward induction to calculate the values at each node in the binomial tree, which is in line with the dynamic programming approach. They also apply the concept of contingent claims to create a replicating portfolio for the underlying asset, i.e. the project itself and from this to obtain the value of the project including the abandonment option and the value of the option to abandon itself. One of the questions that we still need to answer is how to obtain the values for u and d in order to build the event tree that is shown in Fig. 3.10. Copeland and Antikarov (2001b) has developed a method for this, which will be explained in the next section.

3.3 The Portes Case: Copeland and Antikarov

Tom Copeland and Vladimir Antikarov demonstrate their method in *Real Options – A Practitioner's Guide* (2001) using the Portes Case. In this case a firm evaluates the option whether or not to sell its products on the Internet in France. The company and data in this case are fictional.

3.3.1 The Case

Portes develops recovery software and considers to sell the software directly to the business-to-business (B2B) market on the Internet instead of selling it through intermediaries. However, the CEO is hesitant to follow this strategy since the B2B-market in the United States is saturated. A friend from France has informed the CEO that there is a huge demand for the same software as is produced by Portes and that the B2B-market in France is far from saturated. Portes would like to investigate whether it is profitable to invest in the B2B e-commerce in France.

From the NPV-analysis it turns out that the proceeds do not offset the initial costs of $35 million, because this project results in a negative NPV of $319 thousand.

However, the prospects of the B2B-market are too promising to just ignore. Moreover, Portes sees other opportunities as well. They are developing other software that is compatible with the existing software. If the sales of the recovery software follows the expectation, then Portes could decide to sell the additional software on the Internet as well. Since this decision is only made once the sales are successful, and not if sales are unsuccessful, they minimize the downside risk caused by the additional investment. They create their own options, without having the obligation to decide today, and can wait for the moment until more information becomes available. Another option is to sell the entire internet sales platform in case this is not profitable. After making inquiries about this, it turns out that there is a market for internet sales platforms in France too.

Because of all these opportunities, Portes has decided to do a re-appraisal and incorporate the concept of options into their calculations in order to verify whether or not the project is profitable. They will use the method of Copeland and Antikarov to demonstrate this.

3.3.2 The Main Objectives

Reason for the change from NPV to real options is that management of Portes is skeptical about the NPV, since it fails to recognize flexibility and tends to under-value opportunities of the project: this analysis will postulate the advantages of option analysis over the NPV. This expansion has not been incorporated into the NPV-analysis, which of course should be included, in order to have the ability to reduce the risks as much as possible. NPV combines uncertainty to one prediction, because of its static, one-time decision making process. On the contrary, Real Options Analysis does incorporate this uncertainty and enables managerial flexibility to deal with this uncertainty. Therefore the management of Portes is more confident about Real Options Analysis than the NPV analysis.

3.3.3 The Method

The method of Copeland and Antikarov consists of four steps, which will be applied to the Portes case:

1. Compute base case present value without flexibility using discounted cash flow valuation model
2. Model the uncertainty using event trees
3. Identify and incorporate managerial flexibilities creating a decision tree
4. Conduct real options analysis

Copeland and Antikarov (2001c) applies the technique developed by Cox et al. (1979). Cox et al. (1979) use the special structure of recombining trees to model stock price behaviour. The tree of stock prices is used as the underlying value for obtaining the option value. In order to make sure that the modelled stock price in the binomial tree doesn't fluctuate too much, but show the expected standard deviation σ and mean μ of the rate of return concerning the real stock price for each period, Cox, Ross and Rubinstein have derived the following factors for the binomial tree method: $u = e^{\sigma\sqrt{t}}$ and $u = 1/d$. In essence, this means that the stock price itself follows a random walk.

According to Copeland and Antikarov (2001c) this means that a certain variable should follow a random walk. Once we have found the standard deviation σ of the rate of return of this variable, we can obtain the values for u and d. With the values of the up and down factors, u and d, we are able to generate a recombining lattice for the underlying value. In order to meet the requirements of Cox et al. (1979), we will have to make sure that the binomial lattice remains recombining.

The first question is to find the variable that follows a random walk and then to determine the equivalent of the real stock price according to the definition of Cox et al. (1979). To find the answer to this question Copeland and Antikarov (2001c) uses Samuelson's proof. According to Samuelson's proof all different uncertainties, such as demand or price uncertainty, can be combined into one single uncertainty, which is the rate of return and this rate of return will follow a random walk. The possibility to combine all the uncertainties into a single uncertainty is an extremely fortuitous side effect for the Portes case and is therefore applied to this case-study.

This is the so-called consolidated approach developed by Copeland and Antikarov. Unfortunately, it is not always possible to use this approach.

The second question refers to how to define the correct 'value' for the underlying project, i.e. the equivalent of the modelled stock price in the recombining binomial tree. According to Copeland and Antikarov (2001c) the value of the project without flexibility is the best estimate to serve as the underlying project value in order to determine the value of the project with flexibility. In other words, the present value of the project without flexibility is the best unbiased estimate of the market value of the project were it a traded asset. This is also referred to as the Market Asset Disclaimer, or MAD-assumption.

Modeling the value of the underlying asset, i.e. the underlying value of the project without flexibility, involves constructing an event tree. An event tree shows the possible future values of the underlying project under plausible market scenarios. Copeland and Antikarov model such an event tree for the underlying project without flexibility using the recombining binomial tree method and the standard deviation of the rate of return. When we add decision points to the event tree, it becomes a decision tree. This is also called an option valuation lattice, since we have added the option price to the underlying project lattice. Working backward through the decision tree, using the replicating-method to calculate the real options value at each node, we eventually determine the value of the entire project with flexibility to expand, abandon, defer etc. Therefore both the uncertainty and options have been incorporated into the value of the entire project.

The procedure to determine the value of the project consist of four main steps. The first step is to determine the value without flexibility. In the first part of step 2, step 2a, we identify the key drivers of risk that drive the value of a project, and then we quantify and combine them, via a Monte Carlo analysis, into a single uncertainty. This method is justified by Samuelson's proof. In step 2b, we use the volatility in order to determine the up and down movement of the event tree. And from this we are able to model the underlying stochastic process for the project without flexibility. Note that an important property of the classical binomial tree is a recombining tree, therefore the event tree in this example is recombining and should remain recombining. In step 3 we will add the options to the event tree and this in turn will lead to a decision tree. In step 4 we will work backward through this decision tree using the replicating portfolio approach in order to obtain the real options value of the project.

Step 1 Determine NPV

The first step according to the method of Copeland and Antikarov, is a standard net present value analysis of the project using traditional techniques. In this case example we compute the base case present value without flexibility using discounted cash flow (DCF) valuation model. This is already done for the Portes case and it shows a negative NPV of $319 thousand.

The reproduction of the calculation is shown in Fig. 3.13. From this it can be seen that the NPV result is negative and equals $318 thousand instead of $319 thousand. The reason for this little difference is because Copeland and Antikarov

	item	year 0	year 1	year 2	year 3	year 4	year 5	year 6	year 7
1	Quantity (units)		200	230	264	303	348	400	
2	Continuous annual growth rate		13.9%						
3	Price per unit ('000s)		30.00	27.66	25.51	23.52	21.69	20.00	
4	Continuous annual growth rate		-8.1%						
5	Cost per unit		9	8.6	8.1	7.7	7.4	7	
6	Revenues (= [1] x [3])		6,000	6,362	6,735	7,127	7,548	8,000	
7	Costs of goods sold (= [1] x [5])		1,800	1,978	2,138	2,333	2,575	2,800	
8	Gross income (= [6] - [7])		4,200	4,384	4,596	4,793	4,973	5,200	
9	Gross margin		70%	69%	68%	67%	66%	65%	
10	Rent		200	200	200	200	200	200	
11	S&A expenses (= 10% x [6])		600	636	673	713	755	800	
12	EBITDA (= [8] - [10] - [11])		3,400	3,548	3,723	3,881	4,018	4,200	
13	Depreciation (= [19] / 10)		3,500	3,500	3,500	3,500	3,500	3,500	
14	EBIT (= [12] - [13])		-100	48	223	381	518	700	
15	EBIT growth			-148%	368%	71%	36%	35%	
16	Taxes		0	21	84	148	214	280	
17	Net income (= [14] - [16])		-100	27	139	233	304	420	
18	Depreciation (= [19] / 10)		3500	3500	3500	3500	3500	3500	
19	Initial investment	35,000							
20	Free cash flow (= [17] + [18] - [19])	-35,000	3,400	3,527	3,639	3,733	3,804	3,920	
21	Change in FCF			4%	3%	3%	2%	3%	
22	Continuation value								50,960
23	Discount rate	13.8837%							
24	Discount factor (= 1 / (1 + [23])	87.8089%							
25	PV	34,682	36,097	37,582	39,161	40,865	42,734	44,747	
26	NPV (= [21] + [23])	-318	39,497	41,108	42,800	44,598	46,538	48,667	
27	FCF as a % of PV		9.4%	9.4%	9.3%	9.1%	8.9%	8.8%	

Fig. 3.13 NPV analysis of the Portes case

(2001c) doesn't use the exact, but rounded values, which complicates the reproduction of the procedures and calculations. An example of such a practice is performed with the discount rate. The discount rate of 13 %, which they demonstrate in their examples is not the actual discount rate they use in their calculations. The discount rate that is shown in the example is up to 4 decimal places, whereas the exact value for the discount rate is 39496/34681 – 1. When we use a discount rate of exact 13 % in our calculations, the result is a positive NPV and is equal to $1.2 million.

We also face the problem of rounding. In the figures throughout this book we present rounded values, whereas we use non-rounded values for the calculations in Excel. Therefore, demonstrating a calculation and producing that same calculation in Excel using rounded and unrounded values could result in a different outcome. We will ensure consistency between the values in the figures and the outcomes of the calculations. Anyway, we will have to accept that internal inconsistencies for calculations due to rounding will remain to exist.

From the Portes case it can be seen that they face difficulties to estimate the value and therefore use the continuation value of $50.960 for year 7. This value represents all the cash flows after year 6 and therefore is allowed to be discounted on the basis of year 7. Copeland and Antikarov use the following simple growing annuity formula to calculate the continuation value in year 7:

$$continuation\ value = FCF(6) \times (1+g) \times \frac{1}{d-g},\ where$$

g the forecasted growth rate of the free cash flow after year 6
d the expected discount rate

In Fig. 3.13 it is shown that FCF(6) = 3,920. Using similar assumptions as Portes, such as $g = 4\%$ and $d = 12\%$, will result in a continuation value of \$50.960:

$$\$3,920 \times 1.04 \times \frac{1}{12\% - 4\%} = \$50,960$$

The present value (PV) is therefore

$$PV\ (year\ 0) = \sum_{t=1}^{6} FCF\ (year\ t)\ \times\ discount\,factor^{t}$$
$$+\ continuation\ value \times discount\,factor^{7}$$
$$= 3,400 \times 87.8089\ \% + 3,527 \times (87.8089\ \%)^2 + 3,639 \times (87.8089\ \%)^3 +$$
$$3,733 \times (87.8089\ \%)^4 + 3,804 \times (87.8089\ \%)^5 + 3,920 \times (87.8089\ \%)^6 +$$
$$50,960 \times (87.8089\ \%)^7$$
$$= 34,682$$

With an initial investment of \$35,000, we are able to calculate the NPV as follows:

$$NPV = PV\ (year\ 0) - Initial\ investment,$$
$$= 34,682 - 35,000 = -\$318\ thousand$$

Step 2a Add Uncertainty
In this second step we will incorporate uncertainties into the model in order to build the event tree. In this first section we will focus on identifying, quantifying and combining the key drivers of risk into one single uncertainty.

While performing the NPV-analysis, we have made predictions about the future values of the project. Of course, we know that those forecasts do not always correspond with the actual values. For example, the forecast of the price per unit of \$20, could differ from the actual value. In order to assess the accuracy of our predictions we model and study the fluctuation of the price per unit. Different prices per unit result in different NPV's for the project. Running multiple simulations with a different price per unit for each simulation provides the distribution of possible NPV-outcomes for the project. This represents the uncertainty that is incorporated into the project. However, we are not looking for the uncertainty regarding the present value of the project, but are interested in the uncertainty or volatility regarding the rate of return of the project, i.e. the standard deviation regarding the rate of return of the project. This volatility is used to determine the up u and down movement d to construct the event tree, since the rate of return of the project follows a geometric Brownian motion. And knowing that the underlying value follows a geometric Brownian motion, we can apply the Cox-Ross-Rubinstein binomial option pricing model. Copeland and Antikarov (2001c) assumes that the rate of return of a project follows the geometric Brownian motion based on Samuelson's proof. Samuelson's proof shows that properly anticipated prices (or cash flows), i.e. as long as investors have complete information about those cash flows available, fluctuate randomly. This implies that the rate of return of a project always follows the geometric Brownian motion, regardless of the pattern of cash flows that it is expected to generate in the future.

In order to determine the uncertainty of the risk of return, we will first have to define the key drivers of risk, examine and quantify the process followed by these key determinants. From the Portes case it follows that these key drivers are the annual unit sales and the price per unit. Suppose that the annual growth rates of both drivers of risk are normally distributed with a constant mean and standard deviation. This implies, in order to quantify the process uncertainty, that we need to find the mean and standard deviation of this process.

Both means have already been obtained during the NPV-analysis in the previous step (Fig. 3.13): the mean of the growth rate of the price per unit r_p is -8.1 % and the mean of the growth of the annual unit sales r_{Qt} is 13.9 %. These values are based on the unit price and sales in year 6. After all, our analysis is based on the assumption that both variables are normally distributed for each year and a property of the normal distribution is that a stochastic variable with an annual mean of m, a (total) mean for year T of $T \times m$. This results in the following price per unit:

$$\begin{aligned} P\ (year\ 6) &= P\ (year\ 0) \times e^{T \times r_p} \\ &= 30 \times e^{5 \times r_p} = 20 \end{aligned}$$

From this it follows that, $r_p = \frac{\ln\left(\frac{20}{30}\right)}{5} = -8.1\%$. For the annual unit sales we follow the same procedure:

$$\begin{aligned} Qt(year\ 6) &= Qt\ (year\ 0) \times e^{T \times r_{Qt}} \\ &= 200 \times e^{5 \times r_{Qt}} = 400 \end{aligned}$$

So that $r_p = \dfrac{\ln\left(\frac{400}{20}\right)}{5} = 13.9\%.$

In the Portes case, the lower limit of the 95 % confidence interval for year 6 is equal to \$15. This means there is a probability of (100 % – 95 %) / 2 = 2.5 % that the price per unit for year 6 is below \$ 15. Analogously, the lower limit of the 95 % confidence interval for the annual unit sales in year 6 is equal to 190. Now we can determine the standard deviation of both growth rates on the basis of this information of year 6.

For obtaining the standard deviation σ_p of the growth rate of the price per unit, we use another property of the normal distribution. According to this property, annual normal distributed stochastic variables with an annual standard deviation of σ have a (total) standard deviation over T year of $\sigma \times \sqrt{T}$.

On the basis of the lower limits of the 95 % confidence interval, we are able to derive the standard deviation. Note, that the 95 % confidence range for a normal distributed stochastic variable is about two standard deviations above or below the mean, $\mu \pm 2\sigma$.

This means that the price per unit lies between $30 \times e^{(5\times -8.1\ \%)-\ 2\times\ \sigma_p \times \sqrt{5}}$ and $30 \times e^{(5\times -8.1\ \%)+\ 2\times\ \sigma_p \times \sqrt{5}}$ for year 6. We also know that according to Portes the estimate of the lower limit is equal to $ 15.

Thus,

$$30 \times e^{(5\times -8.1\%)-\ 2\times\ \sigma_p \times \sqrt{5}} = 15$$

From this we can derive σ_p, the standard deviation of the growth rate of the price per unit, which is 6.43 %. Analogously, the standard deviation of the growth rate σ_{Qt} of the annual sales per unit is 16.65 %.

We have a mean of −8.1 % and a standard deviation of 6.43 % for the annual growth rate for the price per unit and a mean of 13.9 % and a standard deviation of 16.65 % for the annual growth rate for the annual unit sales. Both annual growth rates are normally distributed. Now we can incorporate both uncertainties, i.e. the price per unit and the annual unit sales. Similarly to Copeland and Antikarov (2001c), in our example, the price per unit depends on the price per unit from the previous year, which is shown below:

$$P(t) = P(t-1) \times e^{r_p}, \textit{ with } r_p \textit{ the annual growth rate of the price per unit}$$

By performing each simulation a draw for r_p (normally distributed with a mean of −8.1 % and a standard deviation of 6.43 %), each time the price, $P(t)$, follows another stochastic process and therefore we have obtained the uncertainty of the price per unit as we wanted. We follow a similar procedure for the annual unit sales.

We can perform multiple simulations and in each simulation we draw an r_p from the sample. Each simulation produces another present value and from this we are able to provide an estimation of the present value of the project. However, we do not need to know the volatility of the present value of the project, but are interested in the volatility of the rate of return r. We will use this value in the next step for the construction of the binomial tree. Since we know that,

$$PV(t) = PV(0) \times e^{r\times t}$$

And for $t = 1$:

$$PV(1) = PV(0) \times e^{r}$$

And for each time we are able to estimate the rate of return r on the basis of year 1 through:

$$
\begin{aligned}
r &= \ln\left(\frac{PV(1)}{PV(0)}\right), \; with \\
PV(0) &= \sum_{t=1}^{7} \frac{FCF(t)}{(1+WACC)^t} \\
PV(1) &= \sum_{t=2}^{7} \frac{FCF(t)}{(1+WACC)^{t-1}} + FCF(1)
\end{aligned}
$$

We can perform these calculations with a program like Crystal Ball © and tell the program that the two normally distributed stochastic variables are the price per unit and the annual unit sales including their parameters. Consecutively, Crystal Ball © performs multiple simulations with the given data and produces the results of the rate of return. Based on these simulations we can calculate the standard deviation σ of the rate of return by Crystal Ball ©. Crystal Ball © produces the results of the simulation and it is shown in Fig. 3.14 that the standard deviation σ of the rate of return is 28.97 %. We follow the results of Copeland and Antikarov (2001c) and we will continue to calculate with $\sigma = 0.30$, which represents the volatility for building the event tree.

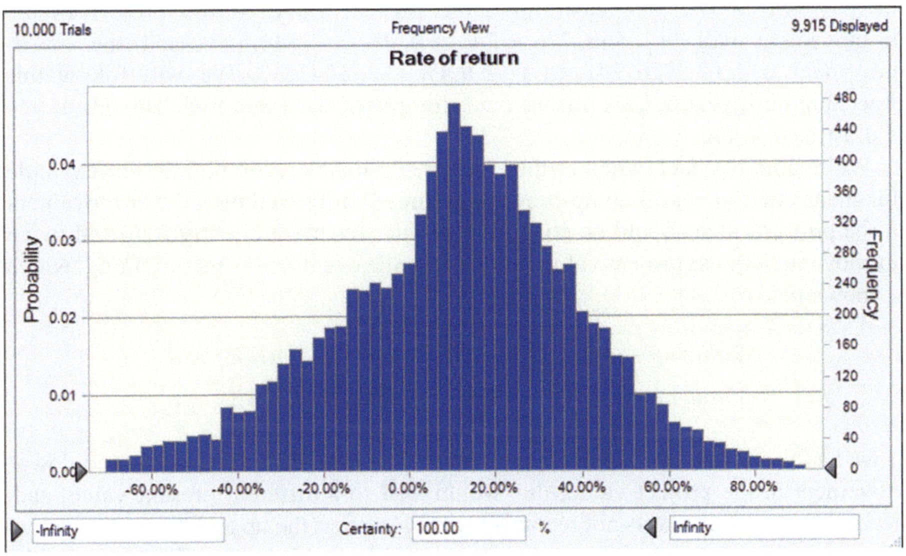

Fig. 3.14 Output of Crystal Ball © for rate of return

Step 2b. Event Tree

Knowing that the volatility of the rate of return is equal to 30 %, we are able to build the underlying asset lattice, i.e. the event tree of the present value of the project. We assume that the volatility remains constant at all time and that $u = e^{\sigma \times \sqrt{T}}$ and $T = 1$ for year 1. From this it follows that $u = e^{0.30} = 1.35$ and $d = 1/u = 0.74$, which is based on the equation of Cox et al. (1979). We'll start with a present value of $ 34, 682 in year 0, which we have obtained in step 1. Copeland and Antikarov (2001c) makes the assumption that there is no volatility in the first year. This is somewhat curious, since the volatility is based on year 1. However, they do not provide any reason for this assumption. Anyway, we will continue with this example of Copeland and Antikarov. The present value of the project in year 1 is $\$34682 \times (1 + \textit{discount rate}) = \$34,682 \times 1.138837 = \$39,497.$ After discounting back the free cash flow, the present value of the project will become $\$39,494 - \$3,400 = \$36,097.$

Next, we're going to extend the analysis to more than one branch, starting with year 2. In year 2 the value for the up-movement is $\$36,097 \times u = \$36,097 \times 1.35 = \$48,726$ and for the down-movement it is $\$36,097 \times d = \$36,097 \times 1.74 = \$26,741$. Normally, having free cash flows means that the tree will no longer be recombining. However, assuming that within the same year the free cash flow is a fixed percentage of the present value of the project, and therefore we do not violate this property. Consequently, we choose the same percentage for the up and down movement, which is the FCF as a proportion of the PV from the NPV analysis that is shown in Fig. 3.13. In year 2 this is equal to $3,527/37,582 = 9.4\%$. After the pay out of the free cash flow, the present value of the project in the up-movement will be $\$48,726 \times (1 - 9.4\%) = \$44,153$ and the down-movement will be $\$26,741 \times (1 - 9.4\%) = \$24,232$. We will follow this procedure until year 6, i.e. until we have completed the event tree. This event tree is illustrated in Fig. 3.15

We're able to check whether the event tree remains recombining. For example this means that in year 3 an up-movement directly followed by a down-movement in the project value should be equal to a down-movement directly followed by an up-movement in the project value. In this case the event tree is recombining, which is shown below:

$$\textit{Value up} - \textit{down}: \; \$36{,}097 \times u \times (1 - 9.4\%) \times d$$
$$\textit{Value down} - \textit{up}: \; \$36{,}097 \times d \times (1 - 9.4\%) \times u$$

If we had used a different percentage for the free cash flow for the up- and down-movement in the project value, this would lead to a different present value, and, hence, lead to a tree that is not recombining. Moreover, the up and down-movement of a recombining binomial tree are neutralized and the only difference in the present value of the project is caused by the free cash flow. After all, with equation $u = 1/d$ the present value of the project after one up followed by one down-movement becomes:

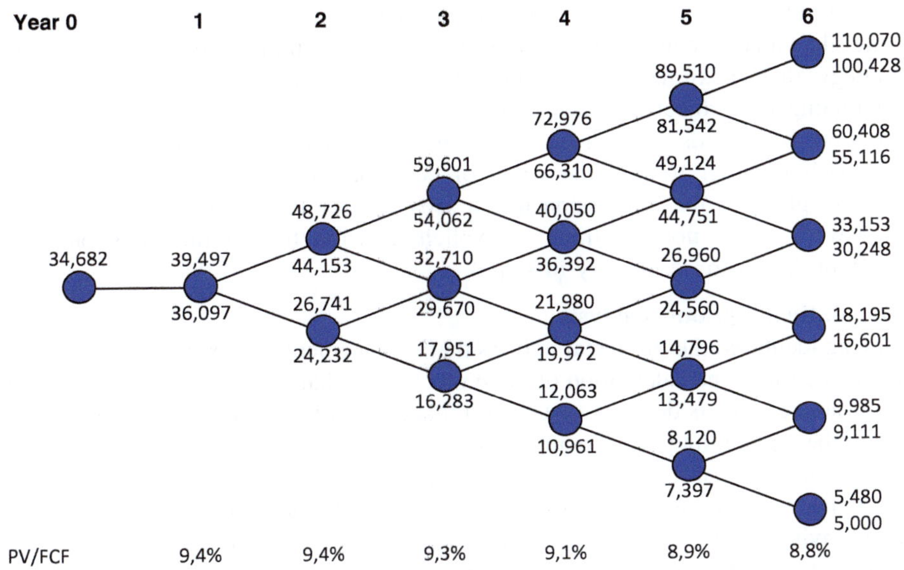

Fig. 3.15 Event tree of the present value of the Portes case (upper value is PV incl FCF, lower value is PV excl FCF)

$$\begin{aligned}\$36{,}097 \times u \times (1 - 9.4\%) \times d &= \$36{,}097 \times (1/d) \times (1 - 9.4\%) \times d \\ &= \$36{,}097 \times (1 - 9.4\%)\end{aligned}$$

By following the aforementioned procedure we have incorporated the volatility into the model and subsequently into the event tree. This is done in order to produce the lattice evolution of the underlying project, still without options.

Step 3. Decision Tree

Since we have constructed the present value of the event tree for the underlying project in step 2, we are able to incorporate the additional options available to management into the model. Portes identifies two options:

- An abandonment put. The entire internet component of the company can be sold for \$ 15 million any time.
- An expansion option. This refers to the introduction of the additional software, which would cost \$ 10.5 million. After implementation, it is expected that this would increase the company's cash flow with 30 %.

The event tree shown in step two, had exactly one present value of the project at each node. In step three we have three values for the project at each node: the value of continuation, abandonment and expansion. The profit-maximizing decision is to make the decision that represents the highest value of the three options (i.e. continue, abandon or expand).

The value of selling is $ 15 million and the value of expansion is (1 + 30 %) times the value of continuing the project minus $ 10.5 million. In order to find the strategy that maximizes the profitability, we'll have to obtain the value of continuing the project for each node of the tree. This is done in step 4, where we work backwards through the binomial tree by using the replicating portfolio approach in order to find the value of continuation. Copeland and Antikarov (2001c) gives us the impression that a separate tree has been built in this step. However, we do not construct an explicit decision tree in this step, but will perform this exercise directly in step 4.

Step 4. Real Options Analysis
Having identified the three real options that management can exercise, we are able to proceed with the calculation of the project value that is based on the underlying asset lattice. This is done in a backward manner, starting from the terminal nodes using the replicating portfolio approach.

Therefore we start at the end node in year 6 and demonstrate the calculation of the upper state that includes only up-movements. The present value of the project after paying out free cash flow is $ 100,428, which is the value of continuing the project (and not the value of expansion or abandonment) as is illustrated in Fig. 3.15. The present value of the project before paying out free cash flow is $110,070, as is presented in the event tree in Fig. 3.15. The value of expansion is then $\$100,428 \times (1 + 30\%) - \$10,500 = \$120,056$ and the value of abandonment is $ 15,000.

The profit-maximizing value at this node is the maximum value of continuation, expansion or abandonment =

$$Max\,(\,\$100,428,\ \$120,056,\ \$15,000\,) = \$120,056, \text{ which means expand}$$

The total present value of the project at this node, the real options value, is this maximum present value plus the free cash flow. We can find the value of the free cash flow in the event tree shown in Fig. 3.15: $\$120,056 + (\$110,070 - \$100,428\,) = \$129,699$. Figure 3.16 shows calculations of these values at each node of the real options value tree in year 6.

We will illustrate the process of reasoning backwards in time using the replicating portfolio approach for the upper node in year 5. The real options value for this node is $ 103,472, which is presented in Fig. 3.16. For illustrative purposes, we show some elements from Figs. 3.15 (event tree) and 3.16 (real options value tree) again in Fig. 3.17.

We'll start with the calculation of the value excluding the FCF, for which we will follow the same approach that was presented in Sect. 3.2.3. Note that Copeland and Antikarov (2001c) uses a risk-free rate of 5 %, which is not explicitly mentioned in their example.

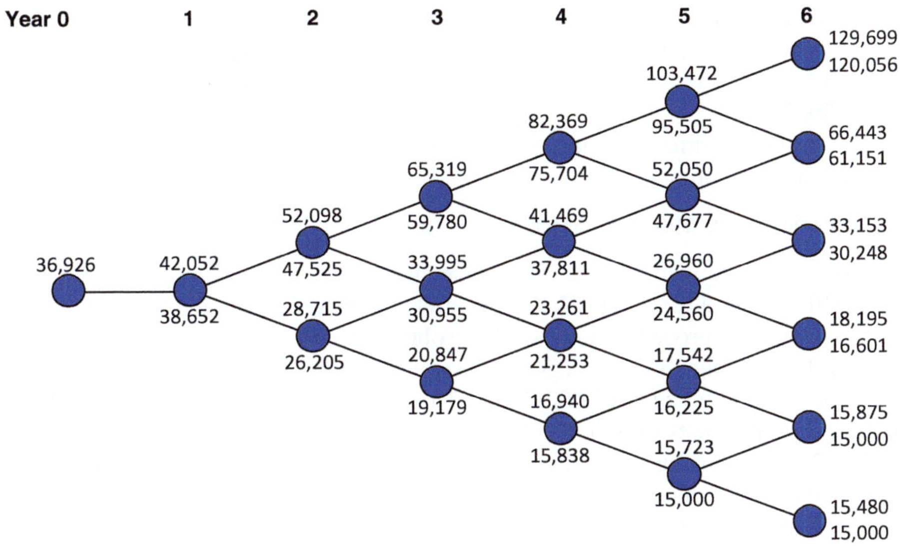

Fig. 3.16 Real option value tree of the Portes case (upper value is PV incl FCF, lower value is PV excl FCF)

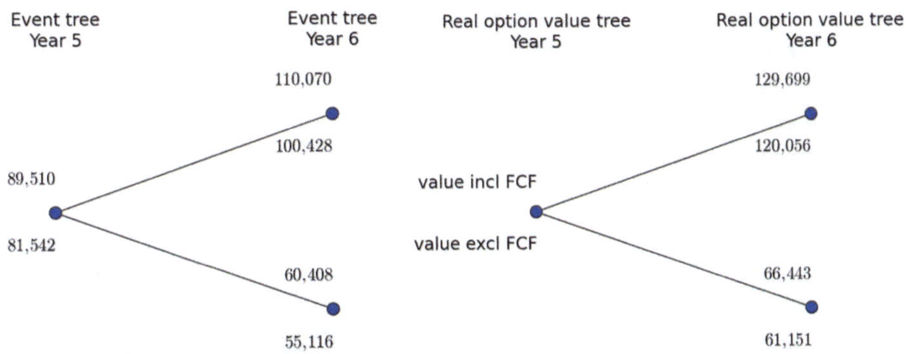

Fig. 3.17 Relevant parts of event tree and real option value tree of the Portes case (upper value is PV incl FCF, lower value is PV excl FCF)

$$m = \frac{\$129{,}699 - \$66{,}443}{\$110{,}070 - \$60{,}408} = 1.27$$

$$B = \frac{\$129{,}699 - m \times \$110{,}070}{e^{0.05}} = \frac{\$129{,}669 - 1.27 \times \$110{,}070}{e^{0.05}} = -9987.91$$

$$\begin{aligned} \mathit{Value\ excl\ FCF} &= m \times \$81{,}542 + B = 1.27 \times \$81{,}542 - 9987.91 \\ &= \$93{,}570 \end{aligned}$$

Since we know the value of continuing the project, we are able to choose the strategy that maximizes the profitability. The value of expansion is $81,542 × (1 + 30%) − $10,500 = $95,505 and the value of abandonment remains $ 15,000.

The profit-maximizing value of this node is the optimal value of continuation, expansion, abandonment:

Max ($93,570, $95,505, $15,000) = $95,505, which means expand

From this we can derive the value including FCF through $95,505 + ($89,510 − $81,542) = $103,472, where the FCF's are obtained from Fig. 3.17.

We repeat this procedure until we have obtained a real options value of $ 42,052 in year 1, as is shown in Fig. 3.16. Discounting this value back to year 0 will result in an amount of $42,052/(1 + 0.138837) = $36,926 for year 0. After deduction of the costs of $35, the real options value becomes $36,926 − $35,000 = $1,926 . This means a positive real options value of $1.9 million, which is over $2 million higher than the NPV, which was −$321 thousand. The flexibility has added $2 million to the project.

Figure 3.18 shows the optimal decisions resulting from the real options analysis. This is a different representation of the optimal exercise of the options in comparison to the real options value tree shown in Fig. 3.16.

3.3.4 Strengths and Weaknesses

The method of Copeland and Antikarov (2001c) is among the most widely used standard methods in real options valuations. Copeland and Antikarov are one of the

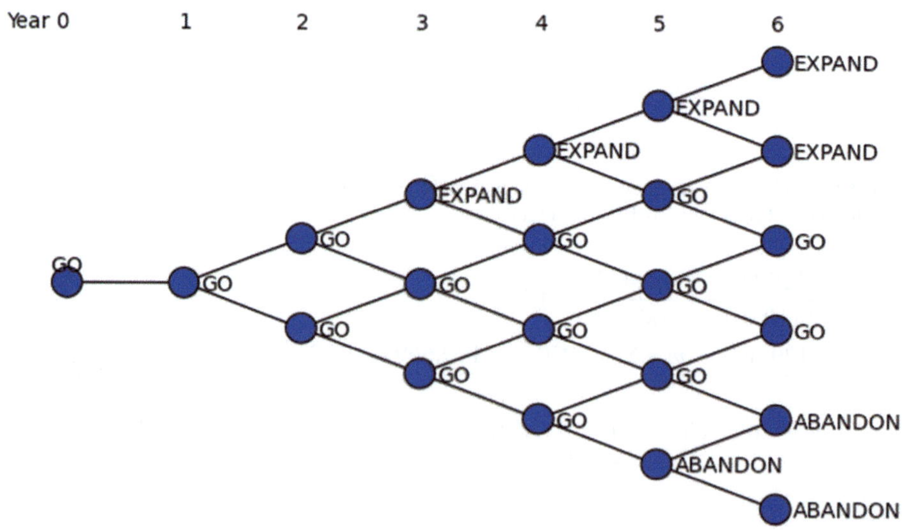

Fig. 3.18 Optimal decision tree of the Portes case

pioneers who have designed a real options approach especially for practitioners. Therefore, many researchers refer to this method for literature review and it is well-respected. Despite their comprehensive introduction to the theme of real options, we weren't able to find literature, which discusses other elements about the strengths of this method than simplicity and completeness of this method. Also, in general, Copeland and Antikarov address the added value of real options analysis, instead of discussing the added value of their method in comparison to other real options methods. The method of Copeland and Antikarov (2001c) has also been criticized because of two assumptions that are used in their model.

One of the key assumptions underlying the approach of Copeland and Antikarov is the so-called Market Asset Disclaimer or MAD, which is the assumption that the present value of the project without options is the best unbiased estimate of the market value of the project were it a traded asset. This means that even if the base case is not marketed we can still build the replicating portfolios, because if it were marketed, the value we calculated would be approximately equal to the publicly traded market value (if it existed). The present value of the project itself, without flexibility, is used as the underlying risky asset, i.e. the twin security, for the replicating portfolio approach. A consequence of this is the subjective estimation of the volatility, as is the case with the Portes case, and therefore the volatility is not determined on the basis of a priced security whose cash payouts in every state of nature over the life of the project are perfectly correlated with those of the project. Portes assumes that $ 15 represents the lower limit of the 95 % confidence range van de price per unit in year 6, which is based on the expertise of the decision makers. Borison (2005) also proposes to look for possibilities to construct the replicating portfolio on the basis of available (realistic) market information. Copeland and Antikarov (2005) acknowledges the proposal of Borison and indicate that whenever a twin security is available this information should be incorporated into the model.

Copeland and Antikarov (2001c) also assumes that the underlying asset follows the geometric Brownian motion. Borison (2005) also questions this assumption, given the fact that the value of the underlying is based on subjective estimations. Copeland and Antikarov justify their assumption on the basis of Samuelson's proof. Samuelson's proof shows that properly anticipated prices (or cash flows), i.e. as long as investors have complete information about those cash flows available, fluctuate randomly. This implies that the rate of return of a project always follows the geometric Brownian motion, regardless of the pattern of cash flows that it is expected to generate in the future. However, Samuelson's prove is based on the assumption that everyone has access to all relevant information and it remains a question whether or not this is true in the 'real' world.

A third objection that Borison has to the use of Copeland and Antikarov's method, is the practical application of the cash flow model that is designed by Copeland and Antikarov and to obtain the subjective input for this model. Borison (2005) concludes that the method of Copeland and Antikarov, together with other real options methods, are unacceptable for the application in practice, despite their user-friendliness.

Other real options literature also questions the volatility estimation method of Copeland and Antikarov (2001c). According to Godinho (2006), this volatility estimation method on the basis of the first time period leads to an overestimation of the volatility. This is corroborated by Haahtela (2011) and Haahtela presents a different solution how to deal with this matter than Godinho (2006).

3.4 The Boeing Approach: Datar Mathews

Vinay Datar and Scott Mathews demonstrate in their paper *A Practical Method for Valuing Real Options: The Boeing Approach* (2007) how Boeing can use real options valuation to decide on whether or not to invest in unmanned aerial vehicles (UAV's). By presenting the real options method as a practical method that management is familiar with, Datar and Mathews have gained the trust from management and therefore were able to start this project. On the basis of their example we will demonstrate the Datar-Mathews method using Crystal Ball © and conclude this section with some literature review about the Datar-Mathews method.

3.4.1 The Case

The market for UAV's seems very promising. On the one hand many monotonous, hazardous, and expensive undertakings could be taken over by UAV's. However, on the other hand there are many risks involved in this market. There is a huge dependence on technological developments, such as aviation control systems, remote sensing and global positioning. It is up to Boeing to decide whether or not to deploy these technologies into the market.

In order to make a decision, Boeing has made the following assumptions. Firstly, a direct R&D-investment of $15 million is needed for the implementation of the technological developments in aviation control systems, remote sensing and global positioning for 2 years. Thereafter, another one-time investment of $325 million is required for the launch of the UAV's. This amount is for development, testing and preparation to be ready for production. Finally, a discount rate of 15 % is used for the calculations.

After the analysis, the project NPV is estimated to be a negative −$19 million, which suggests the project is not worth undertaking. However, the managers overrule this decision and are convinced to have the flexibility to respond to the uncertainties in the market, and therefore are able to complete this project successfully. NPV does not capture the value of flexibility and therefore loses its credibility as a suitable approach. Despite the skepticism about the NPV approach, the managers require a quantitative justification for their choice. The Datar-Mathews method meets the needs of both requirements.

3.4.2 The Main Objectives

The main problem is that managers feel that market uncertainty is not taken into account in the NPV analysis. And their job is to respond to these kind of uncertainties. The NPV analysis combines the multiple scenarios into one most likely scenario. This is not in line with the point of view from the managers. They do see multiple scenarios, where a different decision is made for each scenario.

By incorporating the great diversity of scenarios in this analysis, the method of Datar-Mathews is more aligned with the point of view of the managers and therefore is more accessible to them. Moreover, the Datar-Mathews method is more transparent than the NPV, because the scenarios of this analysis are made explicit. Being accessible and transparent, the Datar-Mathews method is an attractive method for managers.

3.4.3 The Method

The Datar-Mathews method explicitly assumes the various scenarios that are encountered during the project. Firstly, three different scenarios will be provided by the managers, an optimistic, a most likely and a pessimistic scenario. These three scenarios result in three operating profit estimates for each year that form the basis for the real options analysis. In Table 3.3 we can see the forecasts for each of the three scenarios.

From this it can be seen that the investment of $15 million finances the first 2 years of research. Consecutively, in year 2 $325 million is required for the launch of the UAV's. As of year 3 there are three possible cash flows that form the basis for modeling the uncertainty regarding the cash flows. These three estimates can be viewed as representing corners of a triangular distribution, which is a rather basic and understandable distribution of the possible cash flows. The pessimistic scenario represents the minimum cash flow, the most likely scenario represents the mode of the cash flows and the optimistic scenario represents the optimal cash flow, as is illustrated for year 3 in Fig. 3.19 below.

When we perform this procedure for each year, we obtain a series of triangular distributions that represent the evolution of the cash flow uncertainty of the project.

Table 3.3 Cash flows of optimistic, most likely and pessimistic scenarios

Year Scenarios	0	1	2	3	4	5	6	7	8	9
Optimistic		0	0	80	116	153	177	223	268	314
Most Likely		0	0	52	62	74	77	89	104	122
Pessimistic		0	0	20	23	24	18	20	20	22
Launch cost		0	325							
R&D expenses	15									

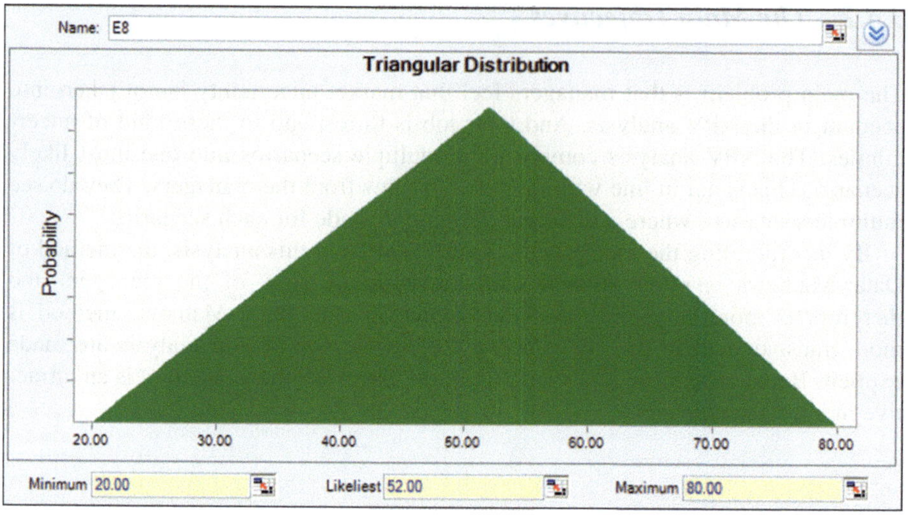

Fig. 3.19 Triangular distribution for year 3 based on cash flows of optimistic, most likely and pessimistic scenarios

With these probability distributions we are able to perform a Monte Carlo simulation. We simulate a possible scenario by drawing a sample from a given probability distribution, where we keep three predefined points of the triangular distribution for each simulation the same. The triangular distribution makes sure that there is a high probability to arrive at the most likely scenario each year. We have also defined a lower and upper limit to the cash flows through an optimistic and a pessimistic scenario.

A simulated scenario consists of a series of yearly cash flows and on the basis of this we are able to calculate the net profit by discounting the cash flows and the launching costs to year 0 and subtract one from the other. In addition, Datar-Mathews discount the launching costs at a rate of 5 %, which results in a cost of $295 million, whereas the cash flows are discounted at a rate of 15 %. This is because managers have more control over the launching costs than over the cash flows. By performing multiple Monte Carlo simulations, we obtain a range of simulated net profits, which is shown in Fig. 3.20.

The net profits and losses for all UAV scenarios collectively determine the real options value for the project, i.e. on the basis of arithmetic mean. However, if the scenario produces a negative outcome, the manager most likely will terminate the project prematurely, and therefore the net profit is zero instead of negative. Therefore all projects with an unsuccessful outcome results in a net profit of zero. Since the enormous R&D investments and the launch costs are in year 0 and year 2 respectively, Datar and Mathews (2007) assumes that managers who expect that the project is unprofitable, will end the project prematurely and therefore will incur no costs. If the manager ends the project, when both the R&D and launch

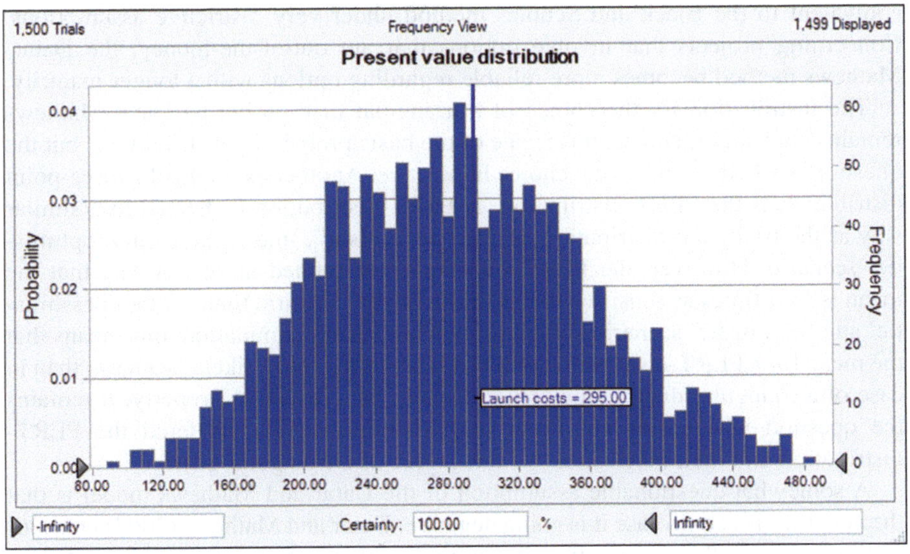

Fig. 3.20 Present value distribution

investments have already been made, the assumption that this does not result in a negative net profit, but still is negative, is highly unlikely.

The real options value from this calculation is \$23 million dollar. After deduction of \$15 million dollar for the R&D investment the project has a value of \$23 million – \$15 million = \$8 million. The real options value is \$ 8 million – – \$19 million = \$27 million higher than the NPV value that fails to value flexibility.

3.4.4 Strenghts and Weaknesses

A great advantage of this method is that it incorporates information, which is already available in most of the companies. And therefore no additional and unknown information is required, which increases the credibility of the valuation. The choice for an optimistic, most likely and pessimistic scenario seems to be logical. Monte Carlo simulation provides a wide range of possibilities to specify the inputs for various probability distributions, which is not the case for methods such as Black and Scholes and Copeland and Antikarov. The Black and Scholes model follows a lognormal assumption, i.e. returns on the underlying are normally distributed, whereas for Datar-Mathews this assumption does not apply. Another reason mentioned by Datar and Mathews (2004, 2007) why this method is gaining acceptance among managers is because of its transparency. Finally, in Datar and Mathews (2004) it is mentioned that this method is especially reliable for projects with options that are in-the-money. Furthermore, the Datar-Mathews method is equivalent to the Black and Scholes method under very restrictive assumptions. Concerning projects that involve options that are out-of-the-money, the Datar-Mathews method becomes more reliable regarding options with a longer maturity.

The justification for the choice of a triangular distribution by Datar-Mathews remains unclear. Of course, this is one of the basic probability distributions, but the question is whether this is best choice in practice. Another example of a three-point distribution is the PERT-distribution. A PERT-distribution is defined in a similar way as the triangular distribution, with a 'pessimistic', 'most-likely' and 'optimistic' scenario. However, the PERT-distribution is defined in such a way that the mean is four times as sensitive to the 'most-likely' scenario than for the 'pessimistic' and 'optimistic' scenario. When using Monte Carlo simulation, this means that the mean for a PERT-distribution will be closer to the 'most likely' scenario than in case of a triangular distribution. This seems to be a desirable property. It remains the question whether or not Datar and Mathews have considered the PERT-distribution and their motivation for the choice of a triangular distribution.

A somewhat questionable assumption of the Datar and Mathews model is that the net profit is zero in case it is going negative. Datar and Mathews (2007) provides justification for this assumption by assuming that management is expected to rationally avoid loss by terminating the project. However, we have noticed that there are huge costs involved in the beginning of the project. Therefore, it is expected that the manager has to terminate the project prematurely in order to have a net profit of zero and no costs. A secondary effect is that the expected NPV will increase, since the negative net profits are artificially kept on zero. The result of this is that the Datar-Mathews model keeps the expected NPV artificially high, what even could lead to a result that an expected negative NPV could suddenly become positive. Another drawback of this method is that simulations are compute intense, require a lot of system resources for processing large computations and therefore could take a long time.

3.5 Parking Garage: de Neufville, Scholtes and Wang

In the paper of de Neufville et al. (2006) a spreadsheet method in Excel ® is designed for valuing real options. The ease-of-use of Microsoft Excel® increases the adoptability for decision makers to use real options analysis to evaluate whether to choose for a flexible or a fixed design in the context of a parking garage. This intuitively appealing approach demonstrates that a flexible design can have great advantages over the fixed design. Firstly, the demand model of the parking garage case example of de Neufville et al. (2006) is discussed. Secondly, a more in-depth explanation is given about the Parking garage case example. Numerical examples and graphical representations will guide real option practitioners through the case example, which enables them to reproduce the entire case example independently. The Microsoft Excel ® spreadsheet, which is provided in addition to the paper by de Neufville et al. (2006) and is publicly available, is gratefully used as a basis for explaining the case-study by de Neufville et al. (2006). The concluding part of this section evaluates the spreadsheet method of de Neufville et al. (2006) and demonstrates a generalized form of the demand model. In Chap. 4, this generalized demand model will be used to demonstrate the impact of a probability distribution on the outcome of the real options value.

3.5.1 The Case

The case deals with a multi-level car park for a commercial center in a region that is growing as population expands. de Neufville et al. (2006) presents the following assumptions regarding the parking garage case example:

- The deterministic point forecast is that demand on opening day is for 750 spaces, and rises exponentially at the rate of 750 spaces per decade;
- Average annual revenue for each space used is $ 10,000, and the average annual operating cost for each space available (often more than the spaces used) is $ 2,000;
- The lease of the land costs $3.6 Million annually;
- The construction will cost $16,000 per space for pre-cast construction, with a 10 % increase for every level above the ground level;
- The site is large enough to accommodate 200 cars per level; and
- The discount rate is taken to be 12 %.
- Land leasing cost ($ 1,800,000 year) is paid upfront at the beginning of each year. No payment is made at the end of the last year.

Additionally, economic analysis needs to recognize that actual demand is uncertain, given the long time horizon. Furthermore, the case assumes that future demand could be 50 % off the projection, either way, and that the annual volatility for growth is 15 % of the long-term average.

Flexibility is created with the expansion option. The owners can design stronger footings and columns to the original building so that they can add additional levels of parking easily. In this particular example, this real cost is assessed as 5 % of the total initial construction cost. The case assumes that no more than 8 levels will be allowed.

3.5.2 The Main Objectives

The objective of de Neufville et al. (2006) is to present an understandable and easy-to-use model for practitioners. In order to do that, the following basic assumptions are used in this method:

- Use of standard, readily available spreadsheet procedures

- Based on data in practice
- Provide graphics that explain the results intuitively

3.5.3 *The Demand Model*

De Neufville et al. (2006) uses an idiosyncratic representation to model the demand uncertainty. Since de Neufville et al. (2006) explains little about this demand model, a more in-depth explanation is provided in this section.

De Neufville et al. (2006) proposes a three-step simulation approach of demand over time. The first step is the deterministic demand projection, which is based on three parameters. The second step consists of simulating three projected realized demands, each drawn from uniform distributions. These three projected realized demands are then used to calculate the projected realized demands for the other years. The final step consists of introducing a second random component, which is used to 'disturb' the projected realized demand profile of the previous simulation step. This is done by drawing growth rates of realized demand in subsequent years, also from uniform distributions. The result is the realized demand, which is used to calculate the NPV.

3.5.3.1 Demand Projection

The deterministic demand projection is the first step for the calculation of the realized demand. This demand projection is based on three parameters, presented in Table 3.4.

Even though de Neufville et al. (2006) states that demand "rises exponentially at the rate of 750 spaces per decade", the Microsoft Excel ® spreadsheet provided by de Neufville et al. (2006) sets the additional demand after year 10 $d_{add\ after\ year\ 10}$ to 250 spaces. Therefore in this case example, $d_{add\ after\ year\ 10}$ is set to 250 spaces as well. The three demand projections are then used to calculate the projected demand for other years according to the following equation:

$$d_t = d_\infty - (d_\infty - d_1)exp(-\beta(t - 1)) \tag{3.15}$$

where d_∞ refers to "final demand" (as t increases):

Table 3.4 Demand projection assumptions

Demand in year 1	750	Spaces	d_1
Additional demand by year 10	750	Spaces	$d_{\text{add\_by\_year\_10}}$
Additional demand after year 10	250	Spaces	$d_{\text{add\_by\_year\_10}}$

$$d_\infty = d_1 + d_{add\ by\ year\ 10} + d_{add\ after\ year\ 10} \tag{3.16}$$

and β is a parameter that is set at a non-negative value via

$$\beta = -\frac{1}{9} LN\left(\frac{d_{add\ after\ year\ 10}}{d_{add\ by\ year\ 10} + d_{add\ after\ year\ 10}}\right) \tag{3.17}$$

Inserting the values of the deterministic demand parameters from Table 3.4 into (3.16) results in the following final demand:

$$d_\infty = 750 + 750 + 250 = 1750$$

Using the same values of the deterministic demand parameters in (3.17) results in the following value for β:

$$\beta = -\frac{1}{9} LN\left(\frac{250}{750 + 250}\right) = -\frac{1}{9} LN\left(\frac{1}{4}\right) = 0.15$$

Inserting the values of d_∞ and β in (3.5) will result in the following demand projection of de Neufville et al. (2006):

$$d_t = 1750 - 1000 exp(-0.15(t - 1))$$

Please note that this demand projection is deterministic. A graphical representation of the demand projection is presented in Fig. 3.21.

3.5.3.2 Projected Realized Demand

In the second step uncertainty is added to the deterministic demand projection. This step consists of simulating three projected realized demands: a projected realized demand in the first year $(\hat{d}_1)$, an additional projected realized demand in

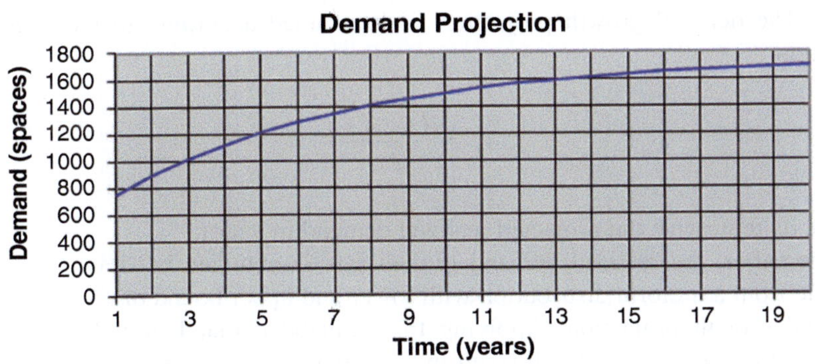

Fig. 3.21 Demand projection

year 10 $(\hat{d}_{add\ by\ year\ 10})$, and an additional projected realized demand after year 10 $(\hat{d}_{add\ after\ year\ 10})$. Each of the three samples are drawn from uniform distributions, with bounds at ±50 percent of the demand projections, i.e. the expectations of the uniform distributions. The three projected realized demands are then used to calculate projected realized demands for other years according to the following equation (note that the same equation is used for the calculation of deterministic demand projection):

$$\hat{d}_t = \hat{d}_\infty - (\hat{d}_\infty - \hat{d}_1)exp(-\beta(t - 1)) \tag{3.17}$$

Suppose the value of parameter $\hat{d}_1$ for demand projection is equal to 750. Then the lower bound of the projected realized demand is as follows:

$$750 - 50\% \times 750 = 750 - 375 = 375$$

and the upper bound is

$$750 + 50\% \times 750 = 750 + 375 = 1125$$

The lower and upper bound of the uniform distribution for parameters $\hat{d}_{add\ by\ year\ 10}$ and $\hat{d}_{add\ after\ year\ 10}$ are obtained in a similar way as parameter $\hat{d}_1$. These three parameters are then used to calculate the projected realized demand for the other years, which result in a similar smooth curve as the deterministic demand projection in step 1.

3.5.3.3 Realized Demand

The final step of the demand model by de Neufville et al. (2006) consists of introducing a second random component, which is used to "disturb" the projected realized demand profile of the second simulation step. This is done by drawing growth rates of realized demand in subsequent years, also from uniform distributions. The demand growth projection is determined according to the following equation:

$$g_t = \frac{\hat{d}_t - \hat{d}_{t-1}}{\hat{d}_{t-1}}$$

where $\hat{d}_t$ represents the projected realized demand in year t.

Thereafter, the realized demand growth rate is obtained by drawing another sample from a uniform distribution with lower and upper bound of 15 % from the demand growth projection. Applying this realized demand growth rate to the projected realized demand will result in the actual realized demand.

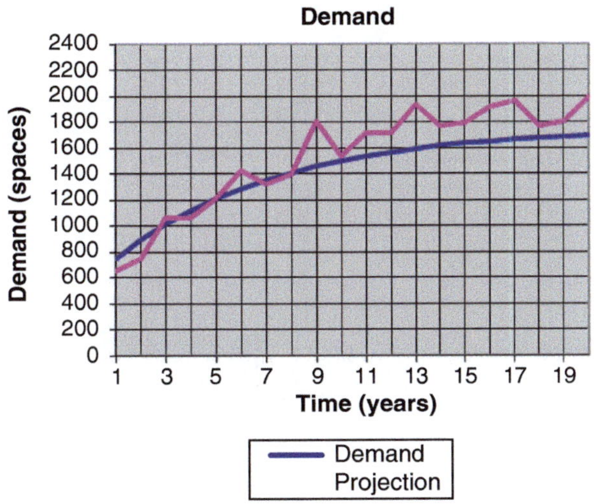

Fig. 3.22 Demand projection

Suppose that the projected realized demand in year 1 is equal to 800 spaces and in year 2 is equal to 880 spaces. The demand growth projection in year 2 is as follows:

$$g_t = \frac{880 - 800}{800} = 10\ \%$$

In order to obtain the value for the realized demand growth rate, a sample is drawn from a uniform distribution with a lower limit of $10\ \% - 15\ \% = -5\ \%$ and an upper limit of $10\ \% + 15\ \% = 25\ \%$. Let's assume that the result of the sample is 20 %, and from this we obtain the value for realized demand in year 2 as follows:

$$realized\ demand_{year2} = 800\ \times\ (1\ +\ 20\ \%) =\ 960\ spaces$$

The second random component, which is used to "disturb" the realized demand profile is clearly visible in Fig. 3.22.

3.5.3.4 Illustration of Demand Model de Neufville et al. (2006)

For illustrative purposes we provide a brief overview of the demand model of de Neufville et al. (2006) in this section.

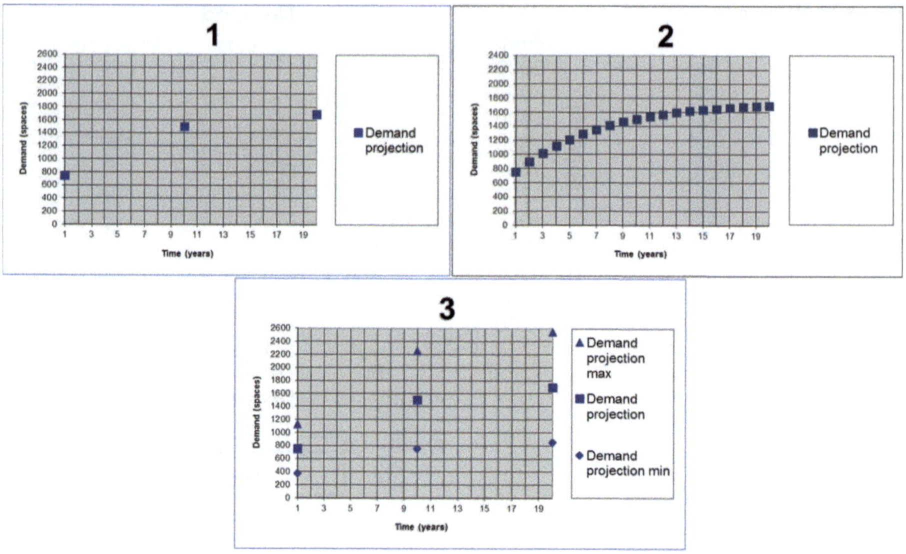

Fig. 3.23 Illustration demand model (1)

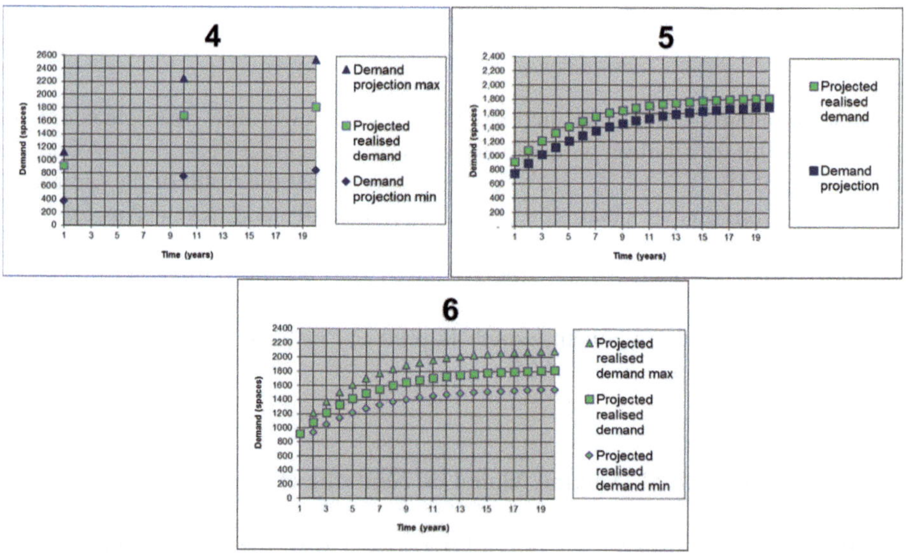

Fig. 3.24 Illustration demand model (2)

The demand model of de Neufville et al. (2006) commences with the demand projection for three time-periods [step 1]. From these three demand projections, the demand projections for the other years are derived through the demand equation [step 2]. Subsequently, for each of the three demand projections from step 1 a lower and upper bound for the uniform distribution are defined [step 3].

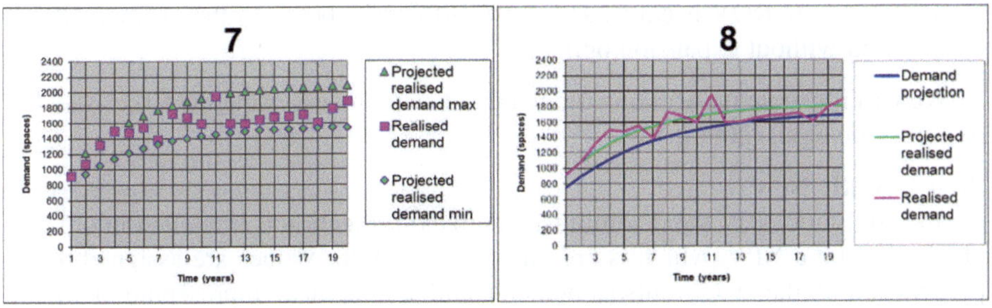

Fig. 3.25 Illustration demand model (3)

Each of the three samples are drawn from uniform distributions, with bounds at ±50 % of demand projection. From this we are able to find the projected realized demand for each of the 3 years [step 4]. Analogously to step 2 we are able to obtain the projected realized demand for each year, with the same demand equation as is used in step 2, but here with the values from step 4 [step 5]. On the basis of the growth rate of the projected realized demand we are able to determine the lower and upper bound of the uniform distribution for each year, which are defined around the projected realized demand from step 5 [step6].

In the final part of this procedure, a draw from a uniform distribution from step 6 is performed for each year in order to obtain the realized the demand for each year in step 7. The demand projection, the projected realized demand and realized demand are combined in the last figure [step 8].

3.5.4 The Method

The method of de Neufville et al. (2006) consists of the following three steps:

1. Determine the optimal design of the parking garage, in case there is no possibility to expand the garage. The optimal design is the design that maximizes the NPV.
2. Recognize the uncertainty in the forecast demand by simulating possible scenarios. Each scenario implies a different NPV. The set of scenarios thus represents the probability distribution of the NPV that might occur and from this the Expected Net Present Value (ENPV) is calculated. For evaluation and illustrative purposes, a cumulative probability distribution is used, from which the summary statistic Value at Risk (VAR) is derived. VAR is a widely used risk measure of the risk of loss on a specific situation. In this case it shows the probability that an NPV might be less or equal to a threshold.
3. Perform a sensitivity analysis in order to evaluate the relation between costs-benefits and the volatility regarding the ENPV of the project. The difference between the maximum ENPV and the NPV of the base case is the value of the flexibility, the real options' value. The decision whether or not to expand is based on the difference between real option value (ROV) and real option cost

(ROC), where ROV is calculated as the difference between the average NPV's with and without expansion option.

We will illustrate the aforementioned three-step process using the Excel-sheet of de Neufville et al. (2006).

Step 1. Static NPV
On the tab Static NPV the deterministic demand projection is modelled in order to obtain the static NPV, which is presented in Fig. 3.26. Values are assigned to the parameters of the deterministic demand and a graphical representation of the demand projection is provided on the tab Static NPV. The highlighted cell in orange on the spreadsheet represents the NPV calculation, which is the result of 20-years discounted cash flows.

The case assumes that no more than 8 levels are allowed. In Table 3.5 different NPV's are presented and from this table we can conclude that the six-level design is the one that maximizes the NPV, which is £ 3.12 million. The NPV calculation in de Neufville et al. (2006) results in a similar NPV as the simulation in this example. However, the NPV results presented in de Neufville et al. (2006) are expressed in dollars by using the exchange rate of 2 dollars for each pound and therefore the maximum NPV in de Neufville et al. (2006) is equal to 2 × £3.12 million = $ 6.24 million.

Step 2. Randomized NPV Simulation
In contrast to step 1, where a deterministic demand model was presented, step 2 and 3 use a stochastic demand model. In step 2, the realized demand is illustrated on the tab Randomized NPV and is illustrated in a similar way as the deterministic demand model on the tab Static NPV. The main difference between the deterministic and the stochastic demand model is the volatility.

Two thousand different scenarios were run and resulted in 2000 different NPV calculations. Based on these NPV's the average standard deviation and 95 % confidence interval are computed. On the tab Randomized NPV Simulation, the average, the standard deviation and the 95 % confidence interval for the design of a 6-level parking garage are shown in Fig. 3.27.

The average NPV of £ 1.44 million euro from the realized demand is much lower than the average NPV of £ 3.12 from the base case. However, a note should be made that the results depend on the simulations. This explains why de Neufville et al. (2006) produces a different average NPV of $2.87 million or £ 1.98 million. This average is quite similar to the results in this example.

De Neufville et al. (2006) demonstrates that a five-level parking garage design results in a higher average NPV, which is £ 1.98 million, than a six-level design. Even though a five-level design generates less cash inflows than a six-level design in case of sufficient demand, the maximum possible loss for a five-level design is less than for a six-level design. This explains the higher average NPV for a five-level design.

This same conclusion can be drawn from the simulation results in our example, only the difference between the average NPV's of the two designs is smaller,

NPV Model for the Parking Garage

Demand projections		
Demand in year 1	750	spaces
Additional demand by year 10	750	spaces
Additional demand after year 10	250	spaces
Average annual revenue	£5,000	per space used
Average operating costs	£1,000	per space available
Land lease and other fixed costs	£1,800,000	p.a.
Capacity cost	£8,000	per space
	10%	growth per level for every level above 2
Capacity limit	200	cars per level
Capacity	5	levels
Time horizon	15	years
Discount rate	12%	

Note: No more than 8

Dynamic demand model:
demand(t) = final demand-alpha*exp(-beta t)
find alpha, beta so that demand (0), demand(10) are as projected

alpha	1000
beta	0.1540327

Year	0	1	2	3	4	5	6	7	8	9	10
Demand		750	893	1015	1120	1210	1287	1353	1410	1458	1500
Capacity	0	1000	1000	1000	1000	1000	1000	1000	1000	1000	1000
Revenue	£0	£3,750,000	£4,465,000	£5,000,000	£5,000,000	£5,000,000	£5,000,000	£5,000,000	£5,000,000	£5,000,000	£5,000,000
Operating costs	£0	£1,000,000	£1,000,000	£1,000,000	£1,000,000	£1,000,000	£1,000,000	£1,000,000	£1,000,000	£1,000,000	£1,000,000
Land leasing and fixed costs	£1,800,000	£1,800,000	£1,800,000	£1,800,000	£1,800,000	£1,800,000	£1,800,000	£1,800,000	£1,800,000	£1,800,000	£1,800,000
Cashflow	£0	£950,000	£1,665,000	£2,200,000	£2,200,000	£2,200,000	£2,200,000	£2,200,000	£2,200,000	£2,200,000	£2,200,000
DCF		£848,214	£1,327,328	£1,565,917	£1,398,140	£1,248,339	£1,114,588	£995,168	£888,543	£793,342	£708,341
Present value of cashflow	£13,441,332										
Capacity cost for up to two levels	£3,200,000										
Capacity costs for levels above 2	£5,825,600										
Net present value	£2,615,732										

Year	11	12	13	14	15	16	17	18	19	20
Demand	1536	1566	1593	1615	1634	1651	1665	1677	1688	1696
Capacity	1000	1000	1000	1000	1000	1000	1000	1000	1000	1000
Revenue	£5,000,000	£5,000,000	£5,000,000	£5,000,000	£5,000,000	£5,000,000	£5,000,000	£5,000,000	£5,000,000	£5,000,000
Operating costs	£1,000,000	£1,000,000	£1,000,000	£1,000,000	£1,000,000	£1,000,000	£1,000,000	£1,000,000	£1,000,000	£1,000,000
Land leasing and fixed costs	£1,800,000	£1,800,000	£1,800,000	£1,800,000	£1,800,000	£1,800,000	£1,800,000	£1,800,000	£1,800,000	£0
Cashflow	£2,200,000	£2,200,000	£2,200,000	£2,200,000	£2,200,000	£2,200,000	£2,200,000	£2,200,000	£2,200,000	£4,000,000
DCF	£632,447	£564,685	£504,183	£450,164	£401,932	£358,868	£320,418	£286,087	£255,435	£414,667

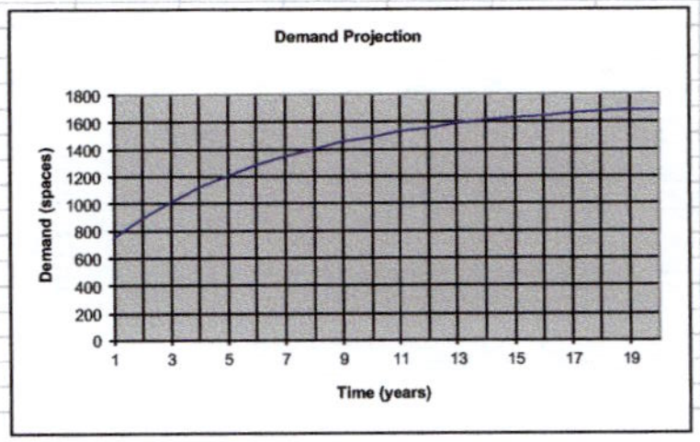

Fig. 3.26 Excel-sheet provided by de Neufville et al. to determine static NPV

Table 3.5 Static NPV per level

Levels	Net present value
1	−£10,210,864
2	−£6,362,173
3	−£2,673,481
4	£615,996
5	£2,615,732
6	£3,119,208
7	£2,022,130
8	−£871,789

Average	£1,435,649			
Standard deviation	£2,811,785			
Average between	£1,372,776	and	£1,498,523	with 95% confidence

Fig. 3.27 Example of randomized NPV

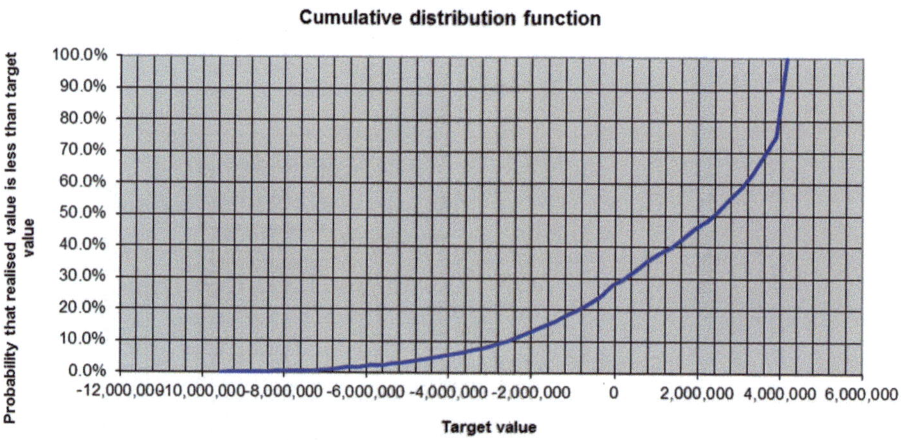

Fig. 3.28 Example of cumulative distribution function of randomized NPV

i.e. $2.87 million for a six-level design versus $2.94 million for a five-level design. The difference of the ENPV between a five-level or a six-level design is too small in order to justify that one design is better than the other. If after 2000 simulation runs it still turns out that the difference of the ENPV between a five and six level design is still insignificant, it's highly unlikely that a six-level design is much better than a five-level design.

In the Microsoft Excel ® spreadsheet by de Neufville et al. (2006), a cumulative distribution of the NPV is presented as the Value at Risk and is illustrated in Fig. 3.28. The Value at Risk is a risk measure to define the level of risk for a given situation or project. Value at Risk indicates the probability of loss expressed in V dollars in a given amount of N days. In the example of de Neufville et al. (2006), N is infinite ($N = \infty$) and the probability for a project loss is about 30 % in case the value of 0. This is illustrated in Fig. 3.28.

Step 3. Expansion Option
The third step describes the expansion of the parking garage. This expansion is discussed on the tab Expansion option of the Microsoft Excel ® spreadsheet by de Neufville et al. (2006) and is quite similar to the tab of randomized NPV. However, the randomized NPV incorporates an additional feature, which is the construction of an additional floor, once the realized demand is higher than the capacity for two consecutive years.

From the results of the simulations of the randomized NPV it turns out that the four-level design maximizes the NPV if we take into account the expansion option. This is because the four-level design reduces the maximum possible loss, but at the same time is able to generate more than the expected demand. In Fig. 3.29 de Neufville et al. (2006) explains the NPV-calculation in order to determine whether or not to incorporate this additional flexibility.

From the results shown in Fig. 3.29, it is recommended to acquire the expansion option, because the real options value of £ 1.550.000 million exceeds the costs of £ 344.800 million. The estimated value for the options embedded in the flexible design is the difference between the expected value of the design with expansion option of £ 3.00 million and the expected value of the design without expansion option (step 2 – five level design). In order to calculate the correct real options value, the same amount of levels for the parking garage design have to be indicated on both the tabs Randomized NPV and Expansion Option. The value of the randomized NPV without expansion option during this simulation was £ 1.45 (for a four-level design and does not match with the results in step two), in this case the real options value is equal to £ 3.00 million – £ 1,45 million = £ 1.55 million. A cumulative distribution of the average NPV illustrates the VaR and is presented in Fig. 3.30. The probability on a project loss has been decreased to a bit above 20 %, whereas in step two with the five-level design without expansion option this probability was about 30 %.

3.5.5 *Strenghts and Weaknesses*

The approach of de Neufville et al. (2006) is designed for estimating the value of real options in engineering systems. This spread sheet model has not been widely discussed in the standard real option literature, but has some commonalities with other simulation approaches such as Copeland and Antikarov (2001a, b, c) and Datar and Mathews (2007).

Average	£2,996,473			
Standard deviation	£3,431,019			
Average between	£2,919,748	and	£3,073,197	with 95% confidence
Real option value	£1,550,363			
Real option cost	£344,800			
Acquire the option?	Yes			

Fig. 3.29 Example of results randomized NPV

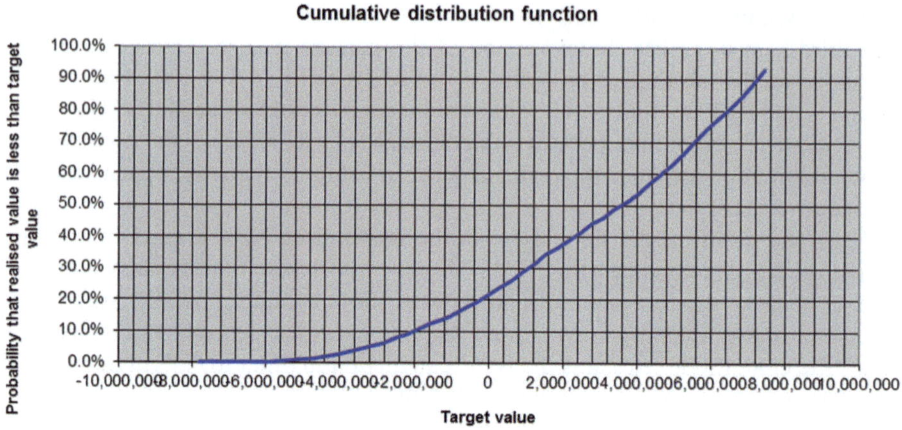

Fig. 3.30 Example of cumulative distribution function of randomized NPV with expansion option

One of the advantages of the method of de Neufville et al. (2006) in comparison to other approaches, is the use of techniques that are well-known by practitioners such as the discounted cash flow model. Furthermore, this method uses standards spread sheet procedures, is based on data readily available in practice and provides graphics that explain the results intuitively. The Microsoft Excel ® spreadsheet is accessible for everyone and therefore practitioners are able to reproduce the results completely, which is a good start to become familiar with the approach.

The spreadsheet approach of de Neufville et al. (2006) is not a widely used approach among practitioners and academics. The reason for this could be the dual nature of Microsoft Excel ®, which is used for the entire process from problem identification to problem solving and visualization. On the one hand, Microsoft Excel ® is quite intuitive and simple to use, but too simplistic for the complex real option problems. It is highly unlikely that a company is willing to make huge investments in a parking garage, where the analysis is solely based on simulations in a Microsoft Excel ® sheet. On the other hand, a stochastic demand model, complex equations, simulations and hidden tables, require advanced modeling techniques in Excel ®. This combination complicates the accessibility and adoptability of a method such as the one of de Neufville et al. (2006). Nevertheless, this intuitively appealing approach could be used as an approximation of the solution. In the context of a parking garage this would mean that a flexible design can have great advantages over the fixed design.

Another main concern of the method of de Neufville et al. (2006) is the demand model. It uses the uniform distribution, one of the basic probability model, and at the same time uses a complex three step procedure for modelling the demand uncertainty. Again, a dual nature of the model. de Neufville et al. (2006) claims that results of the spreadsheet approach provide sufficient evidence to show that a flexible design can have great over the fixed design. And therefore the objective of the method to explain results intuitively is met and no further justification for the choice of this demand model is required. Before corroborating the conclusions of de Neufville et al. (2006), we believe that an in-depth simulation study is required to study the impact of other stochastic models on the choice for a fixed or flexible design. Further to this, we will have to investigate the possibilities to simplify the procedure of the demand model of de Neufville et al. (2006) and to increase the practicality of the model itself. We will address all these matters in Chap. 4.

3.5.6 The Generalized Demand Model

The last point of critics on the model of de Neufville et al. (2006) is that little justification is provided of the impact of the probability distribution for modelling stochastic demand. Linda Peters presents in Peters (2016) a generalized form of the demand model of de Neufville et al. (2006), which enables the possibility to study the impact of probability distribution for modelling stochastic demand. In Chap. 4 we will discuss the design and results of this sensitivity analysis. But first we will discuss the methodology of the generalized demand model itself.

Firstly, we note that the uniform distribution only generates a single expected NPV for the option with expansion and one for the option without expansion. Three different uniform distributions do not have more impact than one uniform distribution. The consequence of this is that the model of de Neufville et al. (2006) leads to only one theoretical outcome for ROV. Furthermore, the demand projection and the growth rate are superfluous and are therefore not incorporated into the generalized demand model.

A more generalized form of the demand model of de Neufville et al. (2006) is created by substituting the uniform distribution by a more generic and flexible distribution, the beta distribution. The beta distribution has two shape parameters that the practitioner can vary with time. With these features the user is able to perform a sensitivity analysis with different probability distributions and study the impact of the results from this analysis.

A disadvantage of the beta distribution is that it has its practical use hampered, because it is not intuitively to directly estimate the shape parameters. In other words, there is no intuitive link between the parameters and the shape of the probability distribution. For this reason, Peters (2016) has performed another substitution, which is the substitution of the beta distribution into the PERT-distribution. As will be discussed later in Chap. 4, the results of the simulation with the PERT-distribution will also have implications on the outcome of the real options model. In this section we will focus on the generalized demand model.

Another additional feature of the generalized demand model is that projected realized demand is based on the realized demand of the previous year, whereas the demand model of de Neufville et al. (2006) produces an entire ex-ante prediction of the realized demand and doesn't provide the opportunity to adjust the demand forecast during the project. Conditioning the model on realized demand of the preceding years, it is possible to incorporate the latest information into the model. The random process of demand is constructed as follows.

3.5.6.1 Distribution of Demand Uncertainty in First Year

Let D_1 denote a random variable for demand in the first year and let B_1 have a beta distribution on the interval (0, 1) with shape parameters $a, \quad b > 0$. We define D_1 as follows:

$$D_1 = (d_1^+ - d_1^-)B_1 + d_1^-$$

where d_1^- and d_1^+ denote lower and upper bounds for demand in year 1, respectively. de Neufville et al. (2006) assume that demand uncertainty is ± 50 % of the demand projection. Peters (2016) follows the same assumptions as de Neufville et al. (2006), which are denoted as follows,

$$d_1^+ = 3d_1^- \tag{3.18}$$

In year 1 expected demand is denoted as follows

$$D_1 = (d_1^+ - d_1^-)\frac{a}{a+b} + d_1^- \tag{3.19}$$

de Neufville et al. (2006) assumes that the expected demand in year 1 is equal to 750. The same assumptions for demand in year 1 are adopted by Peters (2016), for each choice of the values of a and b in the simulations.

Basically, the expectation of the beta distribution is shifted horizontally through (3.19), because the beta distribution is defined on interval (0, 1). This is done in such a way that the expectation of demand is equal to the expectation as is defined in the case study of de Neufville et al. (2006). In addition, a change of scale of the beta distribution is performed in order to use the same intervals that are used by de Neufville et al. (2006).

3.5.6.2 Distribution of Demand from Second Year Onwards

Unlike de Neufville et al. (2006), the model of Peters (2016) is explicitly conditioned on demand of the preceding years. Again, we will proceed with our model on the basis the model of de Neufville et al. (2006). Their "dynamic demand model"

$$d_t = d_\infty - (d_\infty - d_1)\exp(-\beta(t-1)),$$

where d_t denotes realized demand in year t, d_∞ stands for "final demand" (as t increases) and β is a parameter that is set at a non-negative value in de Neufville et al. (2006), is rewritten as:

$$ED_t = cED_{t-1} + (1 - c)ED_\infty$$

where $c = exp(-\beta)$, ED_t denotes the expected demand in year t and ED_∞ denotes the final demand. This expression does explicitly take into account the time-dependency of realized demand of the preceding years. The conditional expectation of demand in year t is constructed as follows:

$$E\left(D_t \middle| D_{t-1}\right) = cD_{t-1} + (1 - c)ED_\infty$$

Peters (2016) uses this as the expectation of a conditional beta distribution in year t, which is specified in a similar way as the distribution of demand in the first year.

3.5.6.3 Illustration Generalized Demand Model Peters

For illustrative purposes we provide a brief overview of the generalized demand model of Peters (2016) in this section. We assume that the practitioner has defined a beta distribution by setting two parameters that may increase or decrease with time.

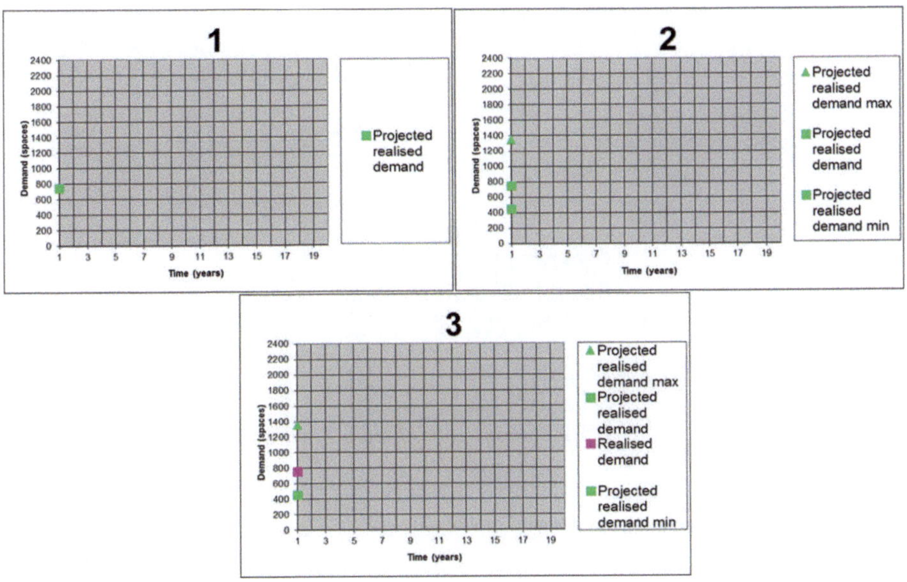

Fig. 3.31 Illustration generalized demand model (1)

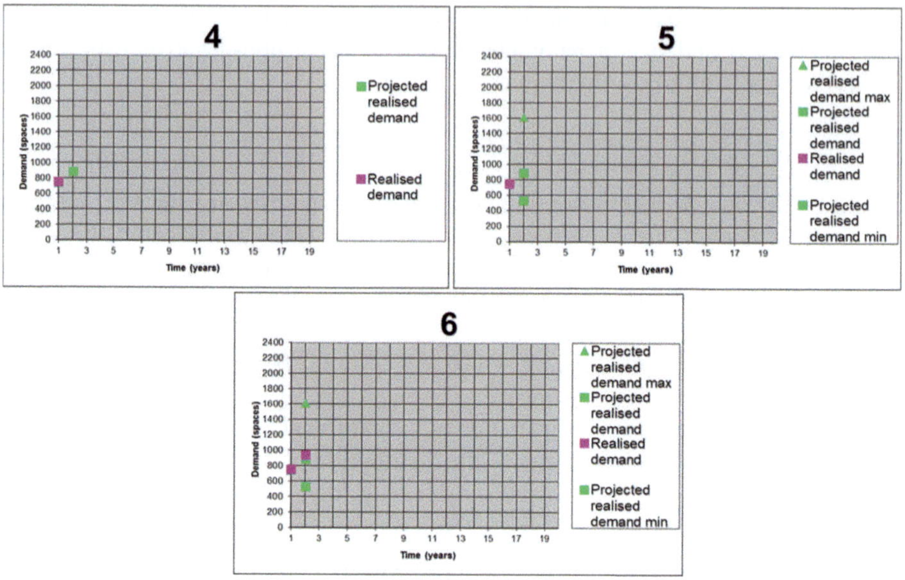

Fig. 3.32 Illustration generalized demand model (2)

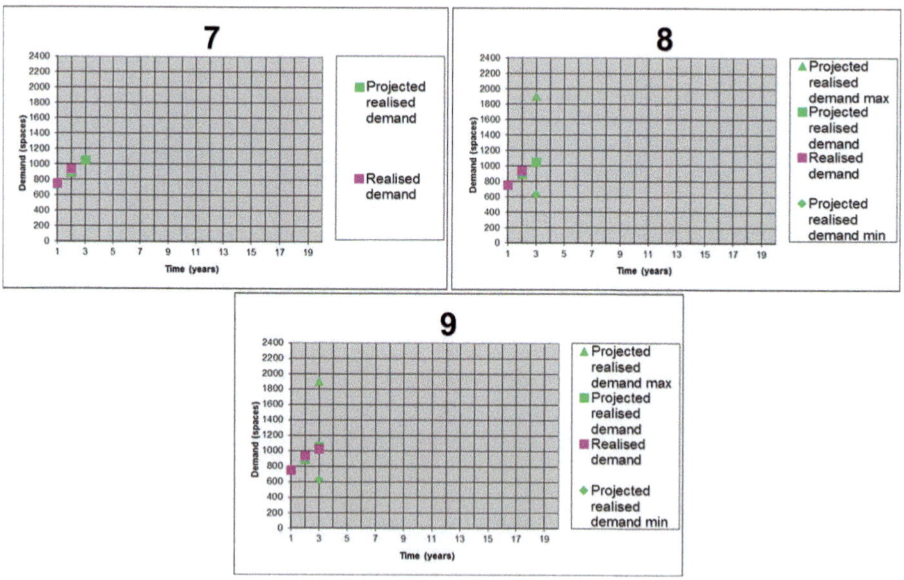

Fig. 3.33 Illustration generalized demand model (3)

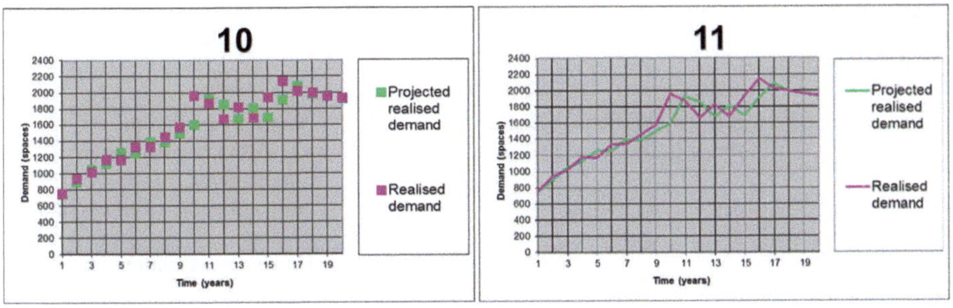

Fig. 3.34 Illustration generalized demand model (4)

The demand model of Peters (2016) commences with the same projected realized demand in year 1 as de Neufville et al. (2006) [step 1]. Subsequently, we define a lower and upper bound for the beta distribution, analogous to de Neufville et al. (2006) [step 2]. A draw from this beta distribution delivers the realized demand for year 1 [step 3].

Based on the realized demand in year 1, we are able to obtain the projected realized demand for next year by using the same demand equation of de Neufville et al. (2006) [step 4]. From this projected realized demand in year 2 we are able to define a lower and upper bound for a beta distribution, analogous to step 2, but now for year 2 [step 5]. A draw from this beta distribution generates the realized demand, analogous to step 3, but now for year 2 [step 6].

We'll repeat this procedure for each year and define the projected realized demand for year 3 [step 7], and again we define the lower and upper bound for a beta distribution [step 8] and conclude with a draw from a beta distribution in order to obtain the realized demand [step 9].

Eventually, we are able to obtain the value for realized demand [step 10] for each year. Both projected realized demand and realized demand are illustrated in Fig. 3.11.

3.6 Summary Real Options Methods

An overview of the different real options approaches, i.e. their objectives and pros and cons, discussed in this book are presented in Table 3.6.

Table 3.6 Summary real options methods

Real options method	Goals	Strengths	Weaknesses
Black-Scholes	Practical closed-form solution	Ease-of-use Used as benchmark	Restrictive assumptions, e.g. GBM and European options only Not applicable to compound options Underlying complex math
Cox, Ross and Rubinstein	Simple derivation Clarify underlying concepts Efficiency	Easy-to-understand European and American options	GBM only Still time-consuming
Copeland and Antikarov	Incorporates volatility into the model Make options explicit	Textbook example of real options analysis	MAD-assumption GBM only Hard to gather required input Volatility overestimated
Datar-Mathews	Make options explicit Easy-to-understand Transparent	Required input already available Not restricted to GBM	Triangular distribution too simplistic Time-consuming ENPV overestimated
de Neufville, Wang and Scholtes	Easy-to-understand To be used in practice	Available and informative spreadsheet	Use of Excel ® Basic demand model

References

Netscape: Black-Scholes

Black F, Scholes M (1973) The pricing of options and corporate liabilities. J Pol Econ 81 (3):637–654

Buckley A, Tse K, Rijken H, Eijgenhuijsen H (2002) Stock market valuation with real options lessons from netscape. Eur Manage J 20(5):512–526

Copeland T, Antikarov V (2001a) Real options a practitioners guide. TEXERE, New York/London

Hull JC (2009a) Options, futures and other derivatives, 7th edn. Pearson Prentice Hall, New Jersey

Marathe RR, Ryan SM (2005) On the validity of the geometric Brownian motion assumption. Eng Econ J Devoted Prob Capital Invest 50(2):159–192. doi:10.1080/00137910590949904

Yen G, Yen EC (1999) On the validity of the Wiener process assumption in option pricing models: contradictory evidence from Taiwan. Rev Quant Finance Account 12(4):327–340. doi:10.1023/A:1008309307499

Option Pricing: Cox, Ross and Rubinstein

Copeland T, Antikarov V (2001b) Real options a practitioner's guide. TEXERE, New York/London

Cox JC, Ross SA, Rubinstein M (1979) Option pricing: a simplified approach. J Financ Econ 1460(7):229–263

Hull JC (2009b) Options, futures and other derivatives, 7th edn. Pearson Prentice Hall, New Jersey

The Portes Case: Copeland and Antikarov

Borison A (2005) Real options analysis: where are the Emperor's clothes? J Appl Corp Finance 17/2:17–31

Copeland T, Antikarov V (2001c) Real options a practitioner's guide. TEXERE, New York/London

Copeland T, Antikarov V (2005) Real options: meeting the Georgetown challenge. J Appl Corp Finance 17/2:32–51

Godinho P (2006) Monte Carlo estimation of project volatility for real options analysis. J Appl Finance 16(1), Spring/Summer p 15–30

Haahtela T (2011) Estimating changing volatility in cash flow simulation-based real option valuation with the regression sum of squares error method. J Real Options 1(1):33–52

The Boeing Approach: Datar Mathews

Datar VT, Mathews SH (2004) European real options: an intuitive algorithm for the black-scholes formula. J Appl Finance 14(1), Spring/Summer 2004 p 45–51

Datar VT, Mathews SH (2007) A practical method for valuing real options: the Boeing approach. J Appl Corp Finance 19(2), Spring 2007 p 95–104

Parking Garage: de Neufville, Scholtes and Wang

Hull JC (2009c) Options, futures and other derivatives, 7th edn. Pearson Prentice Hall, New Jersey

de Neufville R, Scholtes S, Wang T (2006) Real options by spreadsheet: parking garage case example. ASCE J Infrastruct Syst 12(2):107–111

Peters L (2016) Impact of probability distributions on real options valuation. J Infrastruct Syst. doi:10.1061/(ASCE)IS.1943-555X.0000289, 04016005

Chapter 4
The Impact of Probability Distributions

Volatility plays an essential role in real options valuation. In fact, real options models require volatility, which is also the most difficult input parameter to estimate. Higher volatility of the underlying leads to higher real options values. Therefore without volatility, real options provide no additional value for evaluation of investments and therefore it is better to rely on traditional capital budgeting techniques. Thus, when volatility is present, and the higher the better, real options is a very suitable tool for the assessment of investment decisions.

In real options analysis, we model volatility as a random variable using probability distributions. In the previous chapter Copeland and Antikarov (2001) used Geometric Brownian Motion and Datar and Mathews (2007) used the triangular distribution to model volatility. Since volatility is a fundamental parameter in real options valuation, it is even more important to make the right choice concerning the probability distribution of the underlying. However, the methods discussed in the previous chapter mention little about the choice and justification for the probability distribution used in their methods. Furthermore, the authors of these methods do not provide an explanation why they haven't chosen for other probability distributions than the selected one in their models.

In this chapter we will investigate the choice for the type of probability distribution to model the volatility. The paper 'The impact of Probability Distributions On Real Options Valuation (2016)' by Linda Peters will be used for this analysis. This paper demonstrates that the choice of a different probability distribution could result in a different real options value and that even different parameters with the same distribution could produce another outcome of the real options value. Therefore it is seems quite self-evident to select a more generic and flexible distribution for performing a sensitivity analysis than the basic distributions, such as the uniform distribution. However, Peters (2016) does mention that a more flexible distribution could go at the expense of the usability of models and therefore stresses the importance of making an informed choice about the probability distribution and provide a justification for that choice.

L. Peters, *Real Options Illustrated*, SpringerBriefs in Finance,
DOI 10.1007/978-3-319-28310-4_4

4.1 Uniform Distribution, Beta Distribution and PERT-Distribution

In order to demonstrate the impact of probability distributions on the real options value, Peters (2016) has performed a comparative study between three probability distributions: uniform distribution, beta distribution and PERT-distribution. These three probability distributions will be explained in this section.

4.1.1 The Uniform Distribution

The accessibility in order to deal with the uniform distribution mathematically makes this distribution particularly useful in theoretical statistics (Mood et al. 1974). This rectangular distribution is shown in Fig. 4.1.

4.1.2 The Beta Distribution

A random continuous variable is said to have a beta distribution if the function f below is its probability density function (pdf), with shape parameters a, $b > 0$:

$$f(x) = \frac{1}{B(a,b)} x^{a-1}(1-x)^{b-1}, 0 < x < 1 \text{ and zero otherwise}$$

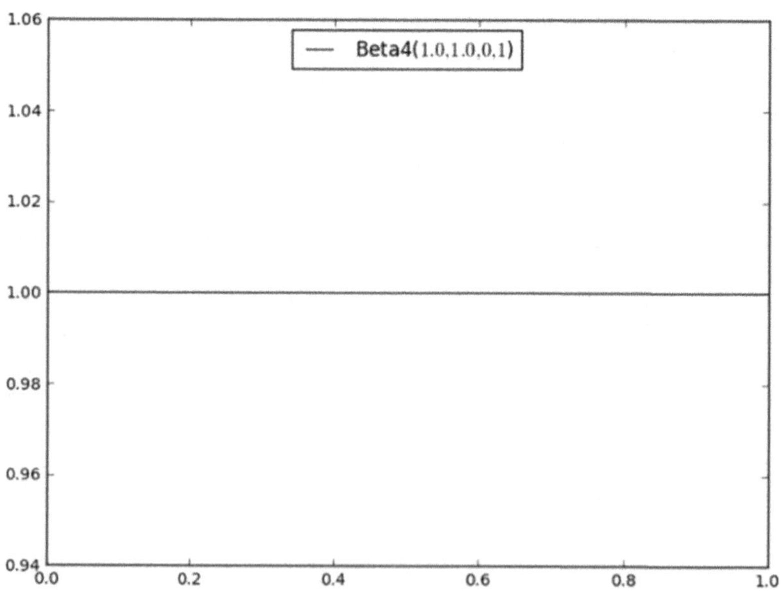

Fig. 4.1 Probability density function of uniform distribution on the interval [0, 1]

$$\text{with } B(a,b) = \int_0^1 x^{a-1}(1-x)^{b-1}dx$$

The parameters a and b are called shape parameters, because these parameters determine the shape of the distribution function, also referred to as the pdf. The pdf is symmetric about its mean when a equals b. If a and b are greater than zero, the mode, i.e. the most likely value, is equal to the mean. When $a < b$ the probability mass tends to shift towards smaller values, whereas if $b < a$ the probability mass tends to shift towards grotere values. The pdf is 'bell-shaped' in case $a, b > 1$ and U-shaped in case $0 < a, b < 1$. When $a = b = 1$ the beta distribution equals the uniform distribution. In other words, the uniform distribution is a special case of the beta distribution. For this reason, the beta distribution is a logical choice for the extension of de Neufville et al. (2006) model, which is modelled with the uniform distribution.

The mean, or expected, value of the distribution is equal to $a/(a+b)$. The mean is equal to ½ when a equals b, less than ½ when $a < b$ and greater than ½ when $b < a$. The variance decreases as a or b increases or both parameters increase.

The following plots illustrate how the parameters a and b shape the probability density function of the beta distribution. The bell-shape in Fig. 4.2 and the U-shape in Fig. 4.3 are easily recognized. Figure 4.4 presents the shape of the pdf for a large value

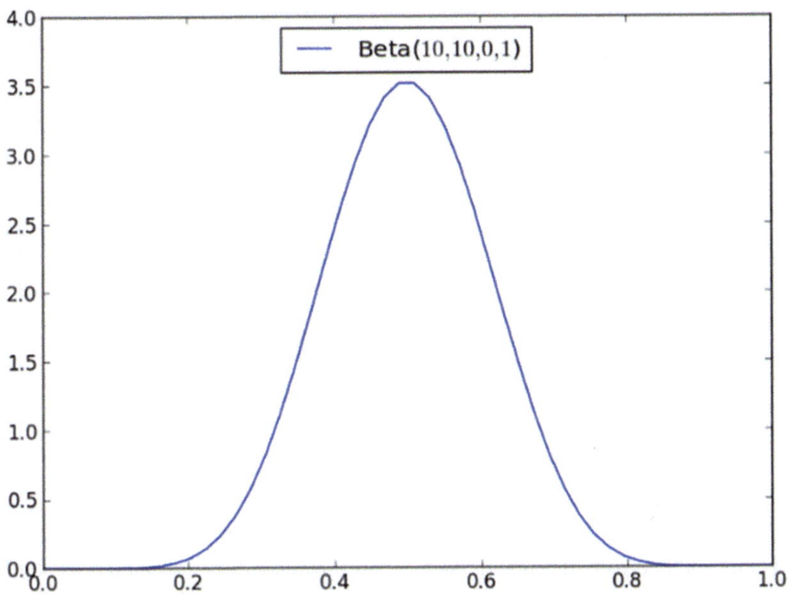

Fig. 4.2 Probability density function of the beta distribution with a = 10 and b = 10

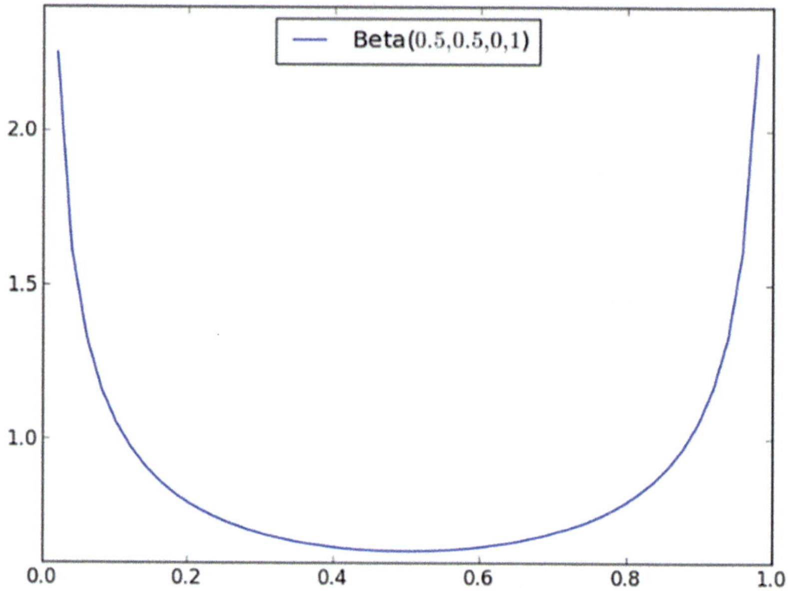

Fig. 4.3 Probability density function of the beta distribution with a = 0.5 and b = 0.5

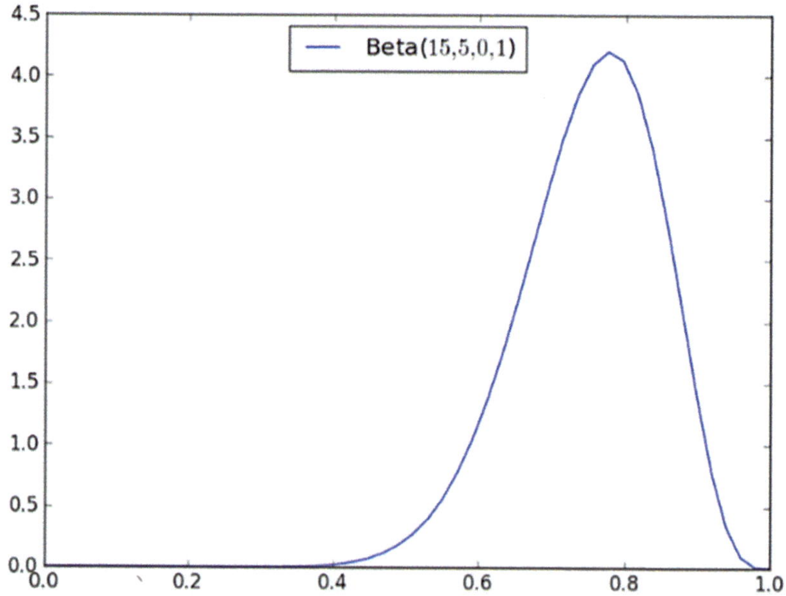

Fig. 4.4 Probability density function of the beta distribution with a = 15 and b = 5

of the mode combined with a longer left tail. The final plot in Fig. 4.5, illustrates a pdf for a small value of the mode, in combination with a longer right tail.

The beta distribution that we have discussed until now had just two shape parameters and was defined on the interval [0,1]. For illustrative purposes, we will call this the beta-2 distribution. It is pretty straightforward to extend the beta-2 distribution by including two additional parameters, a minimum and maximum, to the distribution. This results in a beta distribution with 4 parameters, the beta-4 distribution. One of the disadvantages of both the beta-2 and beta-4 distribution is that both distributions are not intuitive to directly estimate the shape parameters of a and b. This problem is addressed by using the PERT-distribution, where part of the shapes of the beta distribution are covered by the PERT-distribution and represented in a user-friendly way.

4.1.3 The PERT-Distribution

The PERT-distribution is a special case of the Beta-4 distribution and only has three parameters: the minimum, maximum and the mode. This PERT-distribution requires a fixed relation between the shape parameters of a and b of the beta-4 distribution. This enables the use of three instead of four parameters, which have a direct intuitive relationship to the distribution's shape. The related beta-4 distribution should have a unique mode, i.e. $a, b > 1$. When the minimum and maximum values are determined, then all we need to know is the mode in order to specify its related PERT-distribution. Several examples of PERT-distributions are presented in Fig. 4.6.

The PERT-distribution is a practical tool for modeling expert data, because the parameters minimum, mode and maximum could be directly translated from practice. Furthermore, these parameters are easily recognized from the PERT-curve. However, the downside of this practical use is that the PERT-distribution cannot produce all the possible shapes of the Beta-4 distribution and therefore allows for less flexibility than the Beta-4. The PERT-distribution does not cover cases where a and/or b are smaller than 1 (e.g., U-shaped density functions, for which $a, b < 1$). This is called the trade-off between usability and flexibility, meaning the impact of an increased flexibility on the compromises regarding usability and complexity of the model.

4.2 Design Comparative Study Probability Distributions

The demand model of de Neufville et al. (2006) uses the uniform distribution for the modeling of stochastic demand. In order to compare the uniform, beta and PERT-distribution, Peters (2016) has performed two transformations of the demand model of de Neufville et al. (2006). The first transformation is the substitution of the

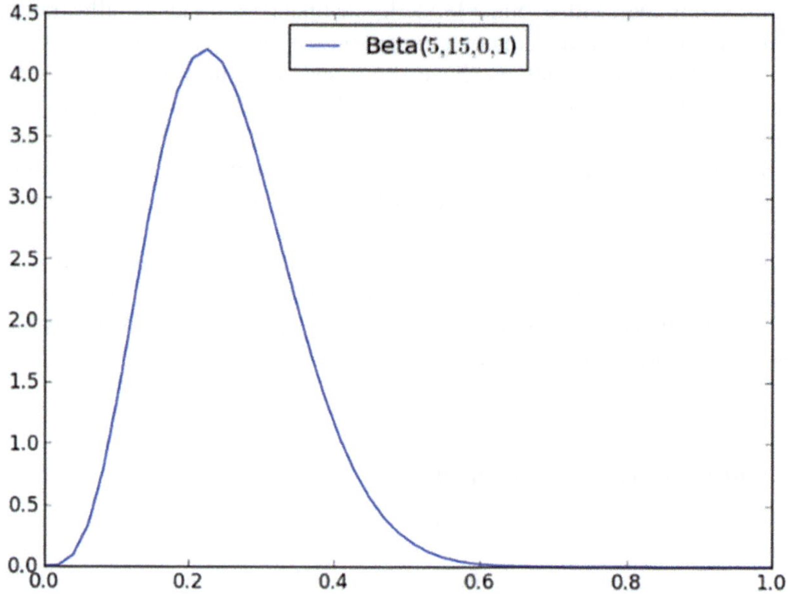

Fig. 4.5 Probability density function of the beta distribution with a = 5 and b = 15

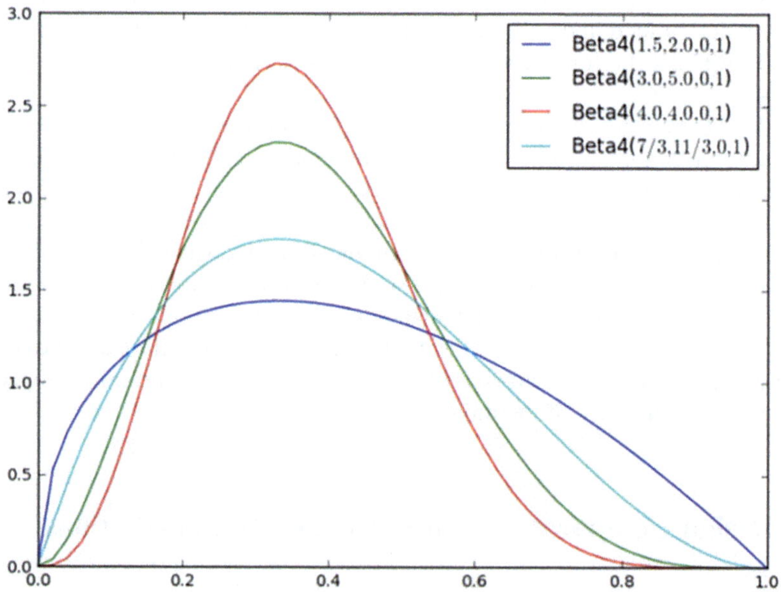

Fig. 4.6 Examples of PERT distribution on the interval [0, 1]

uniform distribution by the beta distribution, which is then followed by a second transformation from the beta distribution into a Pert-distribution. From this we obtain three similar demand models, but a different probability distribution for each model. Now we are able to demonstrate and compare the impact of different probability distributions by using the spread sheet model of de Neufville et al. (2006).

Another feature which Peters (2016) has added to the demand model of de Neufville et al. (2006) are the (non-static) parameters that may increase or decrease with time: parameter a is defined as $a(t)$ and parameter b is defined as $b(t)$. This is done for both the beta and PERT-distribution using change parameters. These change parameters for the beta distribution are defined as c_a and c_b and their impact on parameters $a(t)$ and $b(t)$ is as follows:

$$a(t) = a(1)\exp(-c_a(t-1))$$
$$b(t) = b(1)\exp(-c_b(t-1))$$

Similarly, Peters (2016) has defined the change parameters c_{Min}, c_{Mo} and c_{Max} for the three parameters $Min(t)$, $Mode(t)$ en $Max(t)$ of the Pert-distribution as follows:

$$Min(t) = Min(1)\exp(-c_{Min}(t-1))$$
$$Mode(t) = Mode(1)\exp(-c_{Mo}(t-1))$$
$$Max(t) = Max(1)\exp(-c_{Max}(t-1))$$

Peters (2016) illustrates that more flexible distributions can be generated by just adding change parameters to the underlying probability distributions, which facilitates performing sensitivity analysis.

4.3 Results Simulation Studies

Peters (2016) performs two simulation studies. The first simulation study is conducted by performing multiple simulations with different values for the parameters of the beta distribution using the spreadsheet model of de Neufville et al. (2006). In the second simulation study Peters (2016) performes multiple simulations with different probability distributions using the spreadsheet model of de Neufville et al. (2006). Choosing different parameters or a different probability distribution does have an impact on the real options value and could result in a different outcome. Therefore, the choice for a probability distribution should be carefully considered and studied, before its actual implementation.

Table 4.1 Difference between ROV and ROC for 16 different pairs (a, b) of the beta distribution of demand in year 1

	b = 1	3	5	10
a = 1	-£86,190	-£114,755	-£41,528	£13,508
3	-£12,249	-£2,044	-£40,530	£12,019
5	-£12,629	-£6,847	£3,788	£3,854
10	-£25,416	-£14,965	£31,711	£41,802

4.3.1 *Simulation Results of Different Parameter Values of the Beta Distribution*

In order to have a better and clearer view about the impact of the shape parameters on the decision whether or not to acquire the expansion option we have performed two types of analysis. Firstly, we consider 16 different combinations of parameter values for a and b of the beta distribution of demand in the first year, which covers cases with $a > b$, $b > a$ and $a = b$. In addition, we decrease uncertainty in the demand with time by using the values $c_a = c_b = -0.5$ for each pair (a, b).

For each pair of a and b, the difference between real options value and real options costs is presented in Table 4.1. The results indicate that both types of decisions occur (acquiring the option in green or not acquiring the option in red). Based on the given parameters, the acquisition of the option occurs more frequently when $b > a$, rather than $a > b$. Situations where $b > a$ relate to positively skewed demand distributions and vice versa for situations where a > b, i.e. negatively skewed distributions. The results also suggest that buying the option occurs more frequently when a en b increases.

The simulation results depend on the values of the parameters of the model, i.e. both the parameters for the distribution and other parameters. Peters (2016) has performed a sensitivity analysis in order to demonstrate which parameters have the greatest impact on the real options value. From this analysis it is clearly shown that certain parameters of the distribution have a major impact on the final result, i.e. that different parameters could lead to another decision. For this reason decision makers should be aware of the impact of the shape of probability distributions of uncertainty in demand on decision making. This is one of the main messages that Peters (2016) transmits to the field of real options, which is an important additional insight with respect to the study of De Neufville et al. (2006).

Table 4.2 Summary table comparative study

	Beta vs Uniform				Uniform vs PERT		PERT vs Beta	
	1		2					
	Beta	Uniform	Beta	Uniform	Uniform	PERT	PERT	Beta
ROV - ROC	£777,560	-£241,989	£1,633,139	-£241,989	-£176,477	£1,082,057	£1,082,057	-£568,408
Acquire?	Yes	No	Yes	No	No	Yes	Yes	No

4.3.2 Results Comparative Study of Three Probability Distributions

In the previous section we have performed an individual simulation study with the beta distribution. In addition to this study, we will study the impact of different probability distributions on the acquisition of the expansion option. In this section we will compare the uniform-, beta- and PERT distribution to one another. The results of these four comparative simulations are presented in Table 4.2.

Table 4.2 presents the simulation results of the comparative study between the different probability distributions. The only modification that was performed here is the choice for a different probability distribution given that the models' input parameters remained the same. From this analysis it is clearly shown that a different probability distribution could lead to a different outcome. Based on the results of the comparative study between the beta and uniform distribution, the results of the beta distribution clearly show a higher value for the real options value than its costs and therefore the option should be acquired. This is in contrast to the results of the uniform distribution, which show the opposite. The results of the comparative study between the PERT- and the uniform distribution are analogous to the comparison between the beta and uniform distribution. Furthermore, the more practical version of the beta, the PERT, would lead to different results when compared the results of the beta distribution. This clearly indicates that shapes that can only be produced with the beta distribution should be incorporated into the analysis. To encapsulate the results of this study, decision makers should be aware of the impact of the shape of probability distributions of uncertainty in demand and that the uniform distribution is too basic to describe uncertainty of parking garage demand.

4.4 Conclusion

Peters (2016) has demonstrated that the type of probability distribution for modeling volatility does have a major impact on the real options value. In order to have a better understanding of the impact of probability distributions on the outcome of real options it is necessary to perform a sensitivity analysis. From the results of the sensitivity analysis presented by Peters (2016), we can conclude that the choice for a more generic and flexible distribution, such as the beta distribution, can lead to a different outcome in comparison to a more simple distribution such as the uniform distribution. In case of selecting the more user-friendly Pert-distribution, it again could lead to another outcome. For these reasons, we would advise to study the probability distributions thoroughly, before implementation and not just select a simple distribution for the underlying stochastic variable, such as the uniform distribution, without providing a solid justification for this choice.

References

Copeland T, Antikarov V (2001) Real options a practitioners guide. TEXERE, New York/London

Datar VT, Mathews SH (2007) A practical method for valuing real options: the Boeing approach. J Appl Corp Finance 19(2):95–104, Spring 2007, 477

Mood AM, Graybill FA, Boes DC (1974) Introduction to the theory of statistics, 3rd edn. McGraw-Hill, Inc., New York

de Neufville R, Scholtes S, Wang T (2006) Real options by spreadsheet: parking garage case example. ASCE J Infrastruct Syst 12(2):107–111

Peters L (2016) Impact of probability distributions on real options valuation. J Infrastruct Syst. doi:10.1061/(ASCE)IS.1943-555X.0000289, 04016005

Glossary

@Risk © Risk Analysis Software using Monte Carlo Simulation software developed by Palisade

Abandonment option Option to sell or close down a project (a simple put option). Synonym of option to abandon

Advanced option Antonym of simple option

American option Option that can be exercised at any moment until the maturity date. See Sect. 1.1. Antonym of European option

Analytical method Uses mathematical techniques such as calculus or trigonometry to solve mathematical problems in order to find a closed-form solution. See Sect. 1.5.1. Antonym of numerical method

Arbitrage Opportunity of taking advantage of a price difference between two or more markets. Antonym of no-arbitrage

Bellman equation Necessary condition for optimality to solve mathematical problems using dynamic programming. Synonym of fundamental equation of optimality

Binomial option pricing formula A discrete-time model developed by Cox, Ross and Rubinstein for valuing options. See Sect. 3.2.2.

Binomial tree A tree with exactly two possibilities at each node that represents how an asset price or underlying project can evolve under the binomial model. Most binomial trees in real options analysis are recombining

Black-Scholes formula Closed-form solution developed by Black and Scholes for financial option valuation. See Sect. 3.1.1.

Bonds A long-term debt investment of a firm that obligates the issuer to make specified payments to the holder over a specific period.

Brownian motion Special type of continuous-time stochastic process to model the behavior of stock prices. See Sect. 3.1.1. Synonym of Wiener process.

Call option An option to buy an asset at a certain price by a certain date. See Sect. 1.1. Antonym of put option

Capital budgeting The process of planning and managing a firm's long-term investments

L. Peters, *Real Options Illustrated*, SpringerBriefs in Finance,
DOI 10.1007/978-3-319-28310-4

Cash flow Cash generated by the firm and paid to creditors and shareholders

Closed-form solution For models such as Black-Scholes, where there exist equations that can be solved given a set of input assumptions. See Sect. 1.5.1.

Compound option An option on an option See Sect. 1.1. Synonym of growth option

Contingent claims Approach to option valuation assuming the value of a claim is contingent on an underlying asset. See Sect. 1.5.3.

Continuous-time stochastic process Stochastic process where changes can take place at any time. Antonym of discrete-time stochastic process

Continuation value Value representing uncertain future cash flows. In an option valuation lattice this is the value to continue the existing operations of a project without exercising the option.

Contraction option An option to reduce the scale of a project's operation. Synonym of option to contract and option to scale back

Crystal Ball © Spreadsheet-based application for predictive modeling, forecasting, simulation, and optimization developed by Oracle

Cumulative distribution Describes the probability that a random variable will be less than or equal to x as a function of x. The cumulative distribution function F (x) is given by

$$F(x) = P(X \leq x)$$

Decision tree A graphical representation of alternative sequential decisions and the possible outcomes of those decisions. See Sects. 3.2.5 and 3.3.3

Decision tree analysis Analysis to value a project which takes the flexibility of the project into account. Traditional Decision Tree Analysis, using discounted cash flows, does incorporate flexibility, but fails to adjust the discount rate in order to account for changes in the risk pattern of a project's cash flows. See Sect. 2.3

Deferral option American call option found in most projects where one has the right to delay the start of a project. Synonym of option to defer

Discount rate The rate used to calculate the present value of future cash flows

Discrete-time process Stochastic process where the value of the variable can change only at certain fixed points in time. Antonym of continuous-time stochastic process

Dividend A payment made by a firm to its owners, in the form of either cash or stock

DTA See Decision tree analysis

Dynamic programming Approach to option valuation based on the idea that each decision has both immediate and future consequences. See Sect. 1.5.2.

European option Option that can be exercised only at the end of its life, i.e. at maturity date. See Sect. 1.1. Antonym of American option

Event tree Is intended to model the uncertainty that drives the value of the underlying risky asset through time.See Sect. 3.2.5 and 3.3.3

Exercise price Price at which the holder of an option can buy (in case of a call option) or sell (in case of a put option) the underlying asset. Synonym of strike price

Expansion option An option to make further investments and increase the output if conditions are favorable. Synonym of option to expand, option to scale up and growth option

Free cash flow Cash flow after taxes, interest and all positive NPV opportunities. Synonym of cash flow from assets

GBM See Geometric Brownian motion

Generalized Wiener process Continuous-time stochastic process composed of a constant drift and noise by a Wiener process, which is scaled by a constant factor. A generalized Wiener process is given by $dx = adt + bdz$. See Sect. 3.1

Geometric Brownian motion A stochastic process often assumed for asset prices where the logarithm of the underlying variable follows a generalized Wiener process. Ito-process used in finance and economics to model the behavior of stock prices. The GBM is given by

$$dS = \mu S dt + \sigma S dz.$$

Synonym of random walk. See Sect. 3.1

Geometric series Infinite additive series with a constant ratio between successive terms. See Sect. 1.2

Growth option Option for an early investment that is associated with a greater ability to expand in the future. See Sect. 1.1. Synonym of expansion option, option to scale up and growth option

Hedging Taking a position in two or more securities that are negatively correlated (taking opposite trading positions) to reduce risk

Hedging probabilities Mathematical constructed probabilities to allow cash flows to be discounted at the risk-free rate. See Sect. 2.4. Synonym of risk-neutral probabilities and risk-adjusted probabilities

Fundamental equation of optimality Necessary condition for optimality when solving a mathematical problem by dynamic programming. Synonym of Bellman equation

In-the-money An option whose exercise would produce profits. Either (a) a call option where the asset price is greater than the strike price or (b) a put option where the asset price is less than the strike price. Antonym of out-of-the-money

Interest rate The price paid for borrowing money

Itô calculus Extends the methods of calculus to stochastic processes such as Brownian motion

Itô process Continuous-time stochastic process composed of a variable drift and noise by a Wiener process, which is scaled by a variable factor. An Itô process is given by $dx = a(x,t)dt + b(x,t)dz$. See Sect. 3.1

Jump process Is a type of stochastic process that has discrete movements, called jumps, rather than small continuous movements.

Law of one price Two assets that have exactly the same payouts in every state of nature are perfect substitutes and must, therefore, have exactly the same price (or value).

Log normal distribution A variable that has a continuous lognormal distribution when the logarithm of the variable has a normal distribution.

Long position Position involving the purchase of an asset. Antonym of short position. See Sect. 1.1.1

MAD See Marketed Asset Disclaimer

Marketed Asset Disclaimer Assumption that the present value of the value of the cash flows of the project (asset) without flexibility (i.e. the traditional NPV) is the best unbiased estimate of the market value of the project were it a traded asset. Used by Copeland and Antikarov

Markov process A stochastic process where the behavior of the variable over a short period of time depends solely on the value of the variable at the beginning of the period, not on its past history.

Markov property Refers to the memoryless property of a stochastic process, i.e. a Markov process

Maturity date The end of the life of a contract

Margin requirements Percentage of the value of a security that may be used as a collateral for a loan to finance its purchase

Mean Measure of the central tendency of a stochastic variable or a probability distribution

Monte Carlo simulation A procedure for randomly sampling changes (simulations) in market variables in order to value a derivative such as a real option.See Sect. 1.5.5

Multiplicative process Process in which the value of each state, except for the initial state, equals the value of the previous state multiplied by a constant factor

Net present value The present value of discounted future cash flows minus the present value of the cost of the investment

No-arbitrage No opportunity of taking advantage of a price difference between two or more markets. Antonym of arbitrage

Normal distribution The standard bell-shaped distribution of statistics

NPV See Net present value

Numerical method Uses techniques like Monte Carlo simulation to solve mathematical problems. A method of valuing an option when no formula is available. See Sect. 1.5.1. Antonym of analytical method

Objective probabilities The actual probability that an event will occur

Option A right, but not an obligation, to buy or sell underlying assets at a fixed price during a specified time period. See Sect. 1.1

Option to abandon Option to sell or close down a project. Synonym of abandonment option

Option to contract An option to reduce the scale of a project's operation. Synonym of contraction option and option to scale back

Option to defer Call option found where one has the right to delay the start of a project. Synonym of deferral option

Option to expand An option to make further investments and increase the output if conditions are favorable Synonym of expansion option, option to scale up and growth option

Option to scale back An option to reduce the scale of a project's operation. Synonym of option to contract and contraction option

Option to scale up An option to make further investments and increase the output if conditions are favorable. Synonym of option to expand, expansion option and growth option

Option to switch Are portfolios of American call and put options that allow their owner to switch at a fixed cost (or costs) between two modes of operation. Synonym of switching option

Out-of-the-money Describes an option whose exercise would not be profitable. Either (a) a call option where the asset price is less than the strike price or (b) a put option where the asset price is greater than the strike price. Antonym of in-the-money

Partial differential equation Equation containing partial derivatives of multivariate functions

Present value The current value of future cash flows discounted at the appropriate discount rate.

Probability distribution Function that assigns a probability to each measurable subset of the possible outcomes of a stochastic variable

Put option Right, but not the obligation, to sell an asset for a certain price by a certain date. See Sect. 1.1. Antonym of call option

Random walk Theory that stock price changes from day to day are at random; the changes are independent of each other and have the same probability distribution. An example of this is the Ito-process that is used in finance and economics to model the behavior of stock prices. Synonym of geometric Brownian motion. See Sect. 3.1

Real option Option involving real (as opposed to financial) assets. Real assets include land, plant and machinery.

Recombining binomial tree Binomial tree with the property that multiple paths within the tree end up in the same node, i.e. two or more paths of a tree merge or recombine. A way to restrict the number of nodes in the tree and thereby the number of computations

Recursive equation Equation that should be solved multiple times. The outcome of the equation is dependent on the previous outcome

Replicating portfolio Collection of assets with exactly the same payouts as another collection of assets. Assumes that there are no arbitrage opportunities and that there exist a number of traded assets in the market that can be obtained to replicate the existing asset's payout profile.

Replicating portfolio method Method based on contingent claims. See Sect. 2.4

Risk-adjusted probabilities Mathematical constructed probabilities to allow cash flows to be discounted at the risk-free rate. See Sect. 2.4. Synonym of risk-neutral probabilities and hedging probabilities

Risk-neutral probabilities Mathematical constructed probabilities to allow cash flows to be discounted at the risk-free rate. See Sect. 2.4. Synonym of hedging probabilities and risk-adjusted probabilities

Risk-neutral probability method Method based on contingent claims. See Sect. 2.4

Riskless rate of return The rate of interest that can be earned without assuming any risks.

Samuelson's proof Proof of the theorem that the rate of return on any security will be a random walk regardless of the pattern of cash flows that it is expected to generate in the future as long as investors have complete information about those cash flows.

Security A tradable asset of every kind

Set of equations Mathematical, internally consistent description of a real life problem

Short position A position assumed when traders sell shares they do not own. Antonym of long position. See Sect. 1.1.1

Short selling Selling in the market shares that have been borrowed from another investor.

Simple option Option that is not dependent on other options. See Sect. 1.1. Antonym of advanced option

Standard deviation Measure of the dispersion about the mean of a stochastic variable or a probability distribution. Square root of variance

Standardized normal distribution Normal distribution with mean 0 and standard deviation 1

Stochastic process Collection of random values describing the probabilistic behaviour of a stochastic variable.

Stochastic variable Variable that follows a stochastic process, i.e. a variable whose future value is uncertain.

Stock price Price of a stock

Strike price The price at which the asset may be bought or sold in an option contract. Synonym of exercise price

Switching option Are portfolios of American call and put options that allow their owner to switch at a fixed cost (or costs) between two modes of operation. Synonym of option to switch

Twin security Project with exactly the same payouts as another project. A priced security whose cash payouts in every state of nature over the life of the project are perfectly correlated with those of the project.

Underlying asset Asset on which a contingent claim is dependent

Underlying value Value of the underlying asset

Value at Risk Refers to certain loss that will not be exceeded at some specified confidence level. Single number summarizing the total risk in a portfolio of financial assets, stating that the analyst is X percent certain there will not be a loss of more than V dollars in the next N days

Variance Measure of the dispersion about the mean of a stochastic variable or a probability distribution. Square of standard deviation

Volatility A measure of the uncertainty of the return realized on an asset. Dispersion of a stochastic variable or the measure of the dispersion of a stochastic variable

WACC See Weighted average cost of capital

Weak form of market efficiency Theory that market is efficient with respect to historical price information. In other words past information related to prices is fully reflected in the current market prices and hence it cannot be used to earn excess return.

Weighted average cost of capital Weighted average of the marginal costs of capital after taxes.

Wiener process A stochastic process where the change in a variable during each short period of time of length δt has a normal distribution with a mean equal to zero and a variance equal to δt. Continuous-time stochastic process used in finance and economics to model volatility. See Sect. 3.1.1. Synonym of Brownian motion.

Zero-sum game A situation in which one person's gain is equivalent to another's loss, so that the net change in wealth or benefit is zero.

Index

L. Peters, *Real Options Illustrated*, SpringerBriefs in Finance,
DOI 10.1007/978-3-319-28310-4

MIX
Papier aus verantwortungsvollen Quellen
Paper from responsible sources
FSC® C105338

If you have any concerns about our products,
you can contact us on
ProductSafety@springernature.com

In case Publisher is established outside the EU,
the EU authorized representative is:
Springer Nature Customer Service Center GmbH
Europaplatz 3, 69115 Heidelberg, Germany

Printed by Libri Plureos GmbH
in Hamburg, Germany